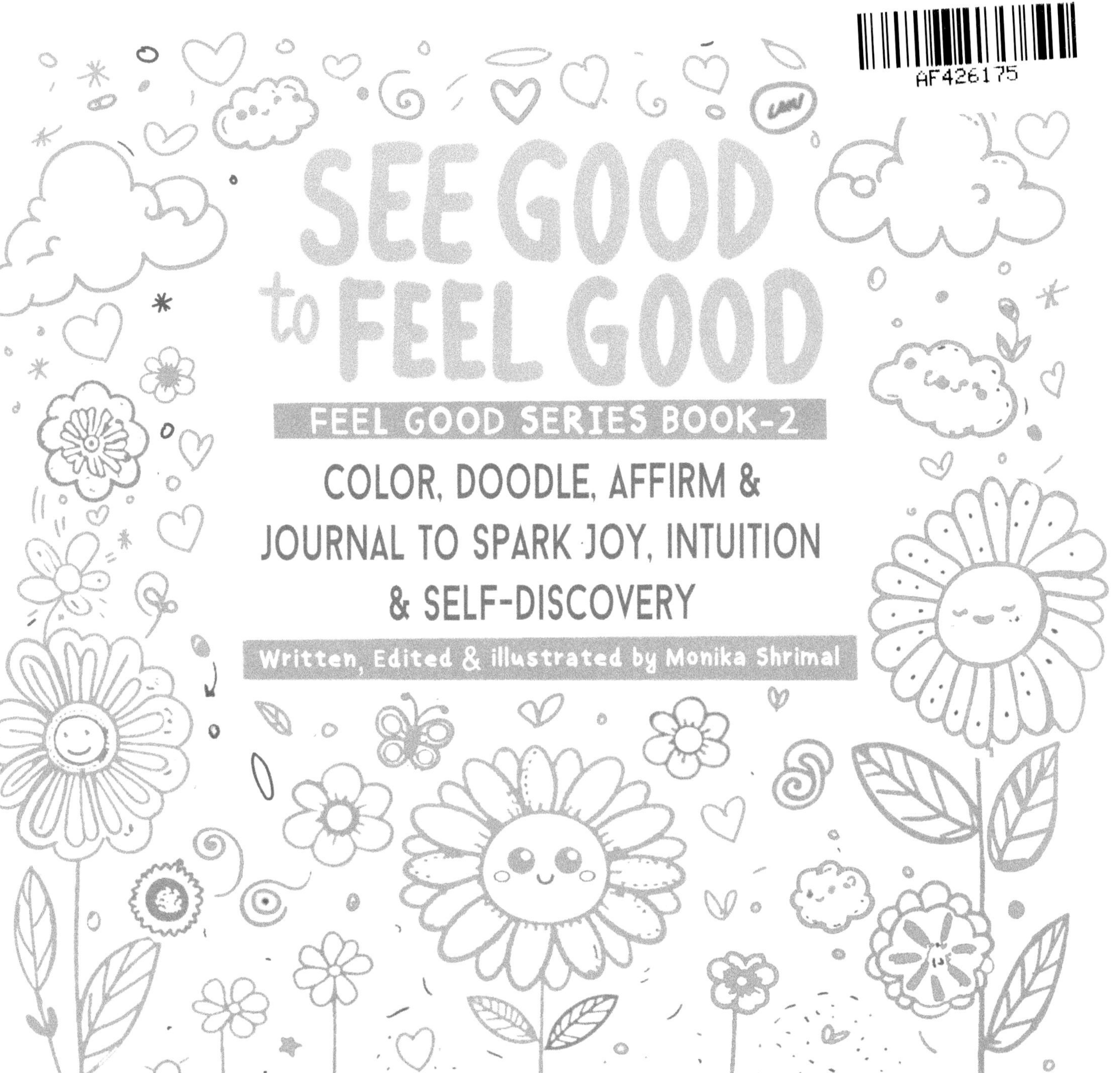

SEE GOOD to FEEL GOOD

FEEL GOOD SERIES BOOK-2

COLOR, DOODLE, AFFIRM &
JOURNAL TO SPARK JOY, INTUITION
& SELF-DISCOVERY

Written, Edited & illustrated by Monika Shrimal

Grateful to-

Parents, siblings, family, in-law family, friends, readers, acquaintances, various tribes and communities, school teachers, spiritual gurus, yoga teachers, nature, kids, and various book authors. Special thanks to two favorite people, sister Namrata and especially husband Naman, for standing by, throughout ups and downs and for his invaluable help in editing this book and bringing these dreams to life.

Welcome Message

Dear Reader,

Welcome to the second book in the Feel Good Series, designed to spark joy, nurture your intuition, and guide you on a path of self-discovery. This book combines the power of affirmations with the creative expression of coloring, doodling, affirmation & journaling to help you appreciate yourself, build positive habits, and stay present in the moment. Whether you are an experienced artist or new to drawing, this journey is yours to explore at your own pace. Let each page inspire you to see the good in yourself and the world around you.

How to Use This Book

1. Daily Practice: Each day, read the affirmation, reflect on it, and then engage with the coloring & doodling prompt. Use your creativity to complete the doodle and add color.

2. Self-Reflection: Take a moment to jot down any thoughts or feelings that arise. This space is for you to explore and express your inner world.

3. Be Present: Focus on being in the moment as you draw and color. Pay attention to your breathing, thoughts, and sensations.

4. Celebrate Wins: Whenever you catch yourself doing something right, take a moment to acknowledge and appreciate it. This practice will help you build the habit of seeing the good in yourself and others.

5. Flexible Approach: There is no right or wrong way to use this book. Feel free to skip around, revisit favorite pages, or take your time with each section. This is your journey, so make it uniquely yours.

Materials Needed

- Drawing Supplies: Pencils, pens, markers, or any other drawing tools you prefer.
- Coloring Tools: Colored pencils, crayons, watercolors, or markers for adding color to your doodles.
- Notebook or Journal: For additional reflections and notes.
- Comfortable Space: A quiet, comfortable place where you can relax and focus.

Setting Intention

Before you begin, take a moment to set a personal intention for your journey with this book. Here are a few steps to help you get started:

1. Find a Quiet Space: Sit comfortably in a quiet place where you won't be disturbed.

2. Breathe Deeply: Take a few deep breaths to center yourself and bring your attention to the present moment.

3. Reflect on Your Goals: Think about what you hope to achieve through this journey. Do you want to increase your self-awareness, build a habit of mindfulness, or simply enjoy a creative outlet?

4. Set Your Intention: Write down your intention at the beginning of the book. It could be something like, "I intend to embrace joy and self-discovery through daily journaling, coloring, doodling and affirmations."

Example Intention

My Intention:

"I intend to embrace the present moment, appreciate my strengths, and cultivate a habit of seeing the good in myself and others. Through this journey, I aim to nurture my creativity and connect deeply with my inner self."

Conclusion

This book is your companion on the path to joy, intuition, and self-discovery. Embrace each page with an open heart and mind, and allow the process to unfold naturally. Enjoy your journey!

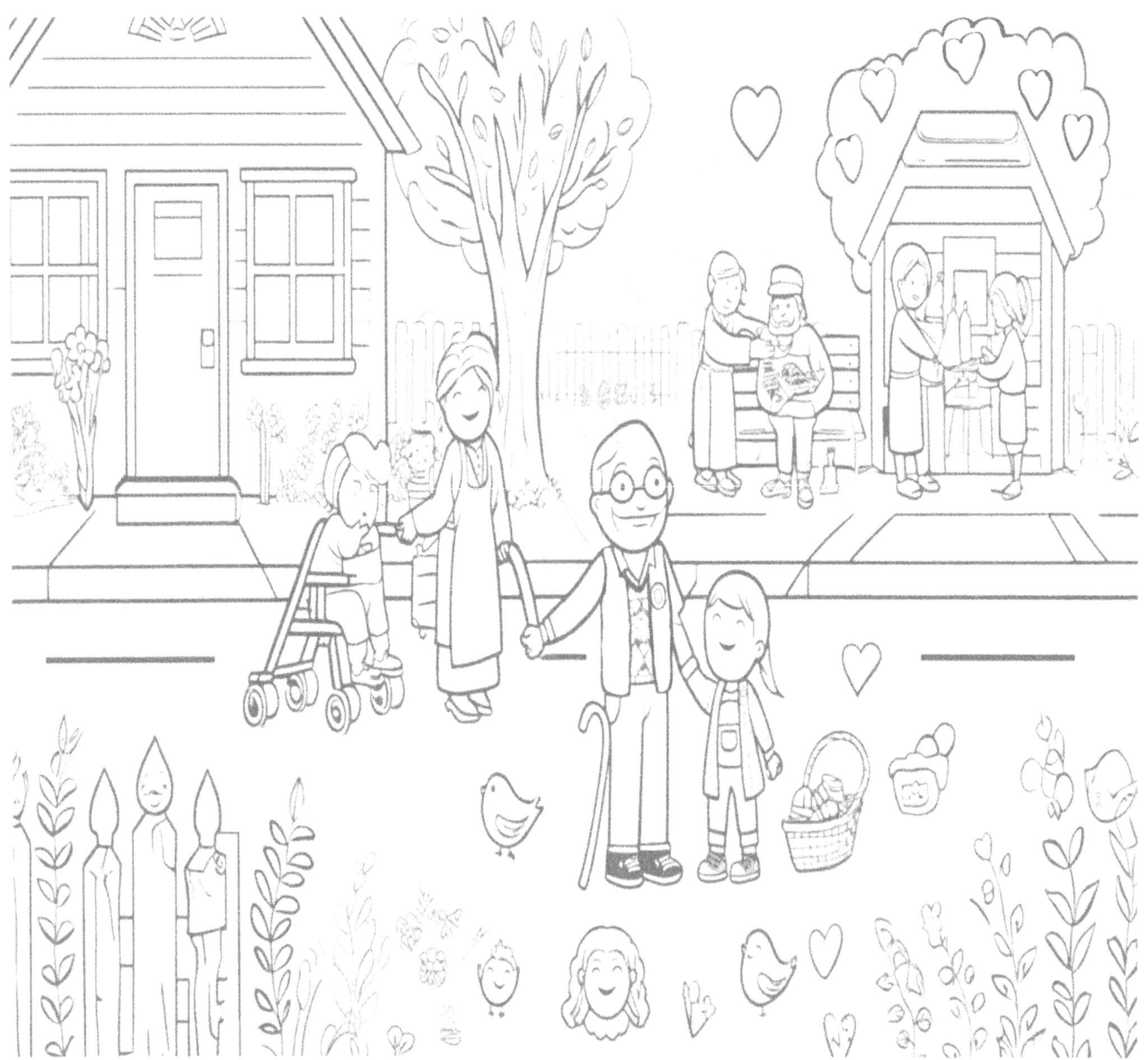

What did you notice first in this piece of art?? Take a moment to look deeply. Can you accept and appreciate this art & parts of it, coloring it as a whole?

Which parts of you and others are unacceptable ? List 5 ways to embrace & accept yourself and others as a whole with love.

I embrace and appreciate myself and others as unique and whole, with love and compassion.

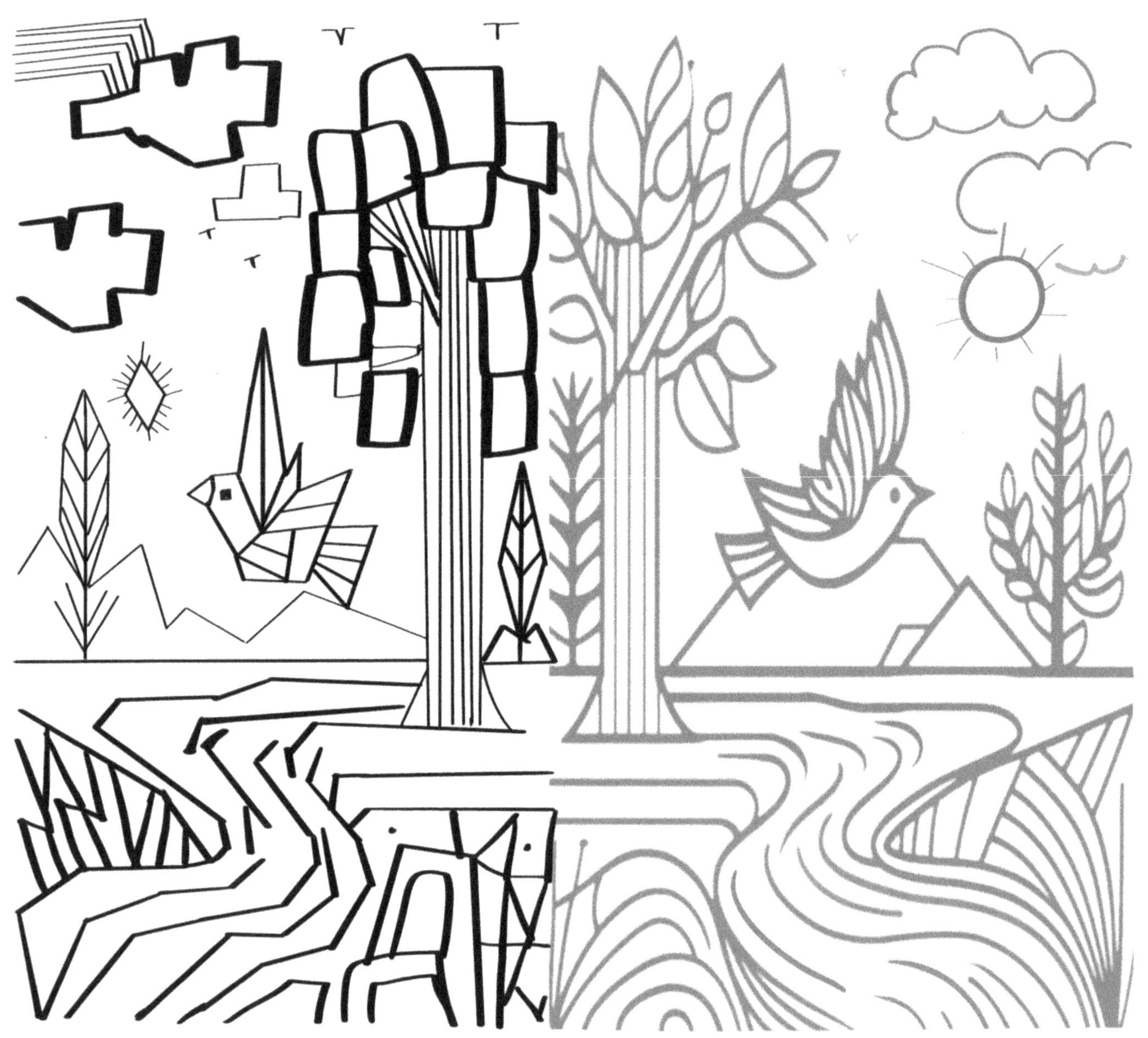

Which art is more beautiful ?
Perfect & geometrical   OR   flowing, real , imperfect & artistic
which one or both would you like to appreciate it by coloring ??

Where have you been perfect & controlling? List 5 ways you can let go of perfection & embrace imperfection.

I let go & let flow

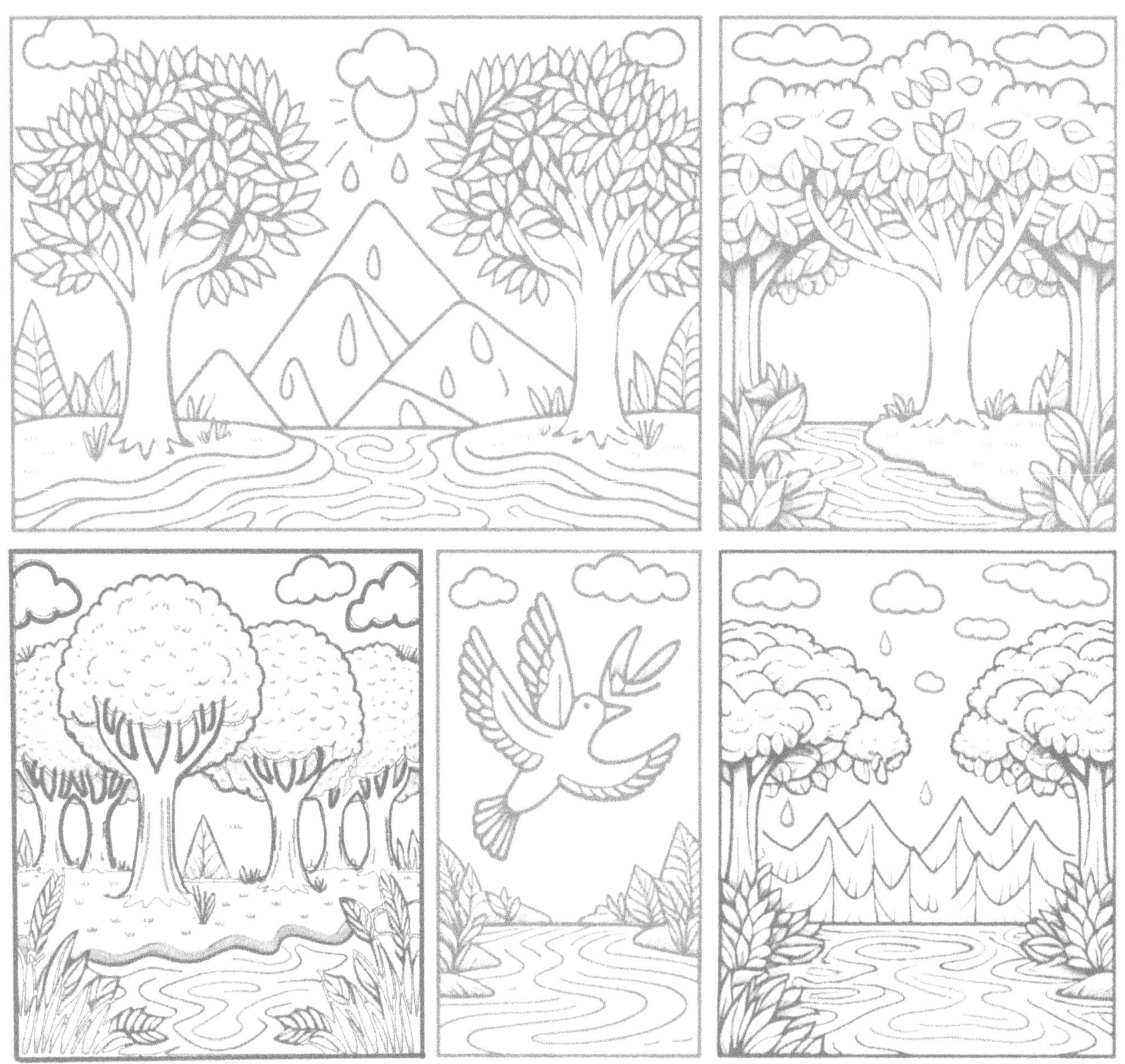

What do you most like about nature ? Can you color those parts or whole of the image you really appreciate & like?

List at least 5 parts of you & others (select one person you dislike) that you can appreciate & like.

I focus on & appreciate the best in myself & others, allowing it to grow.

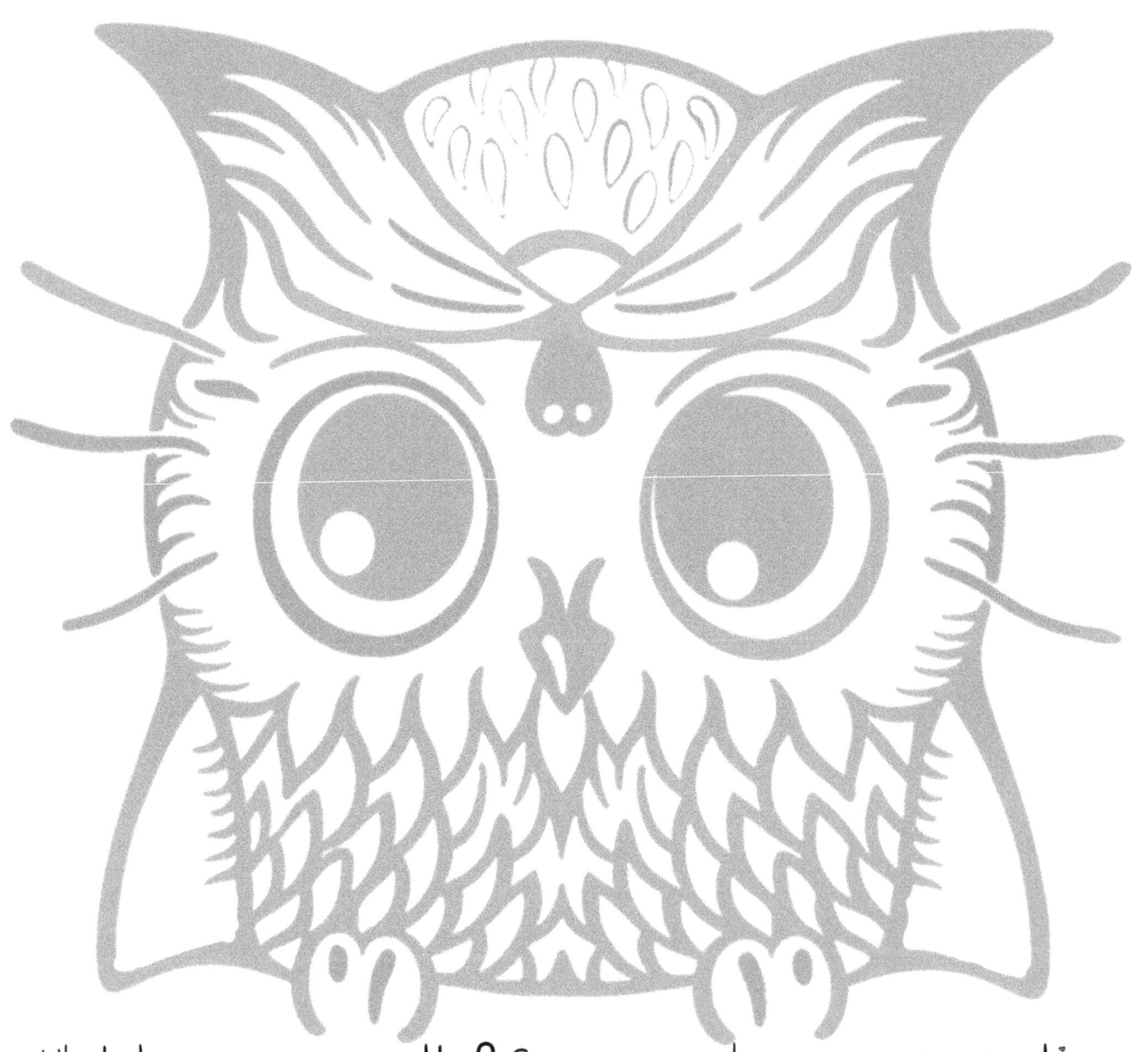

What do you see currently ? Can you see change your perspective & Color it?

Where in your life you dislike something or someone or yourself or situation ? List ways you can look at it in a new perspective.

I always see situations, things and people from a positive perspective.

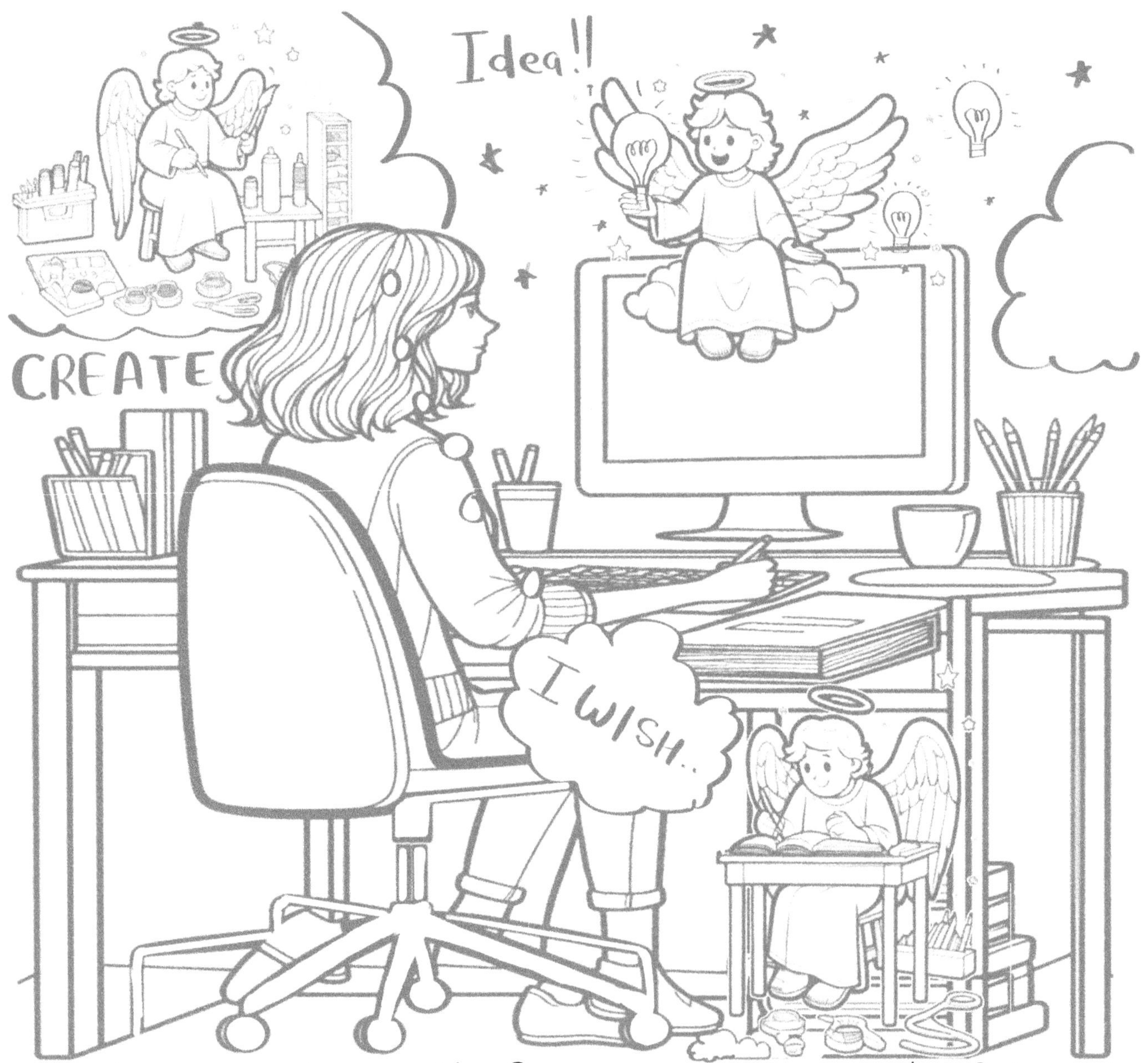

Was it your creation or idea? Can you see so many helpful angels around you and appreciate and name them with colour?

Where in your life you disregarded your own efforts or help from others ? List ways to appreciate your own efforts & help from angels that look like human around you.

I always accept, value & appreciate efforts of myself and others.

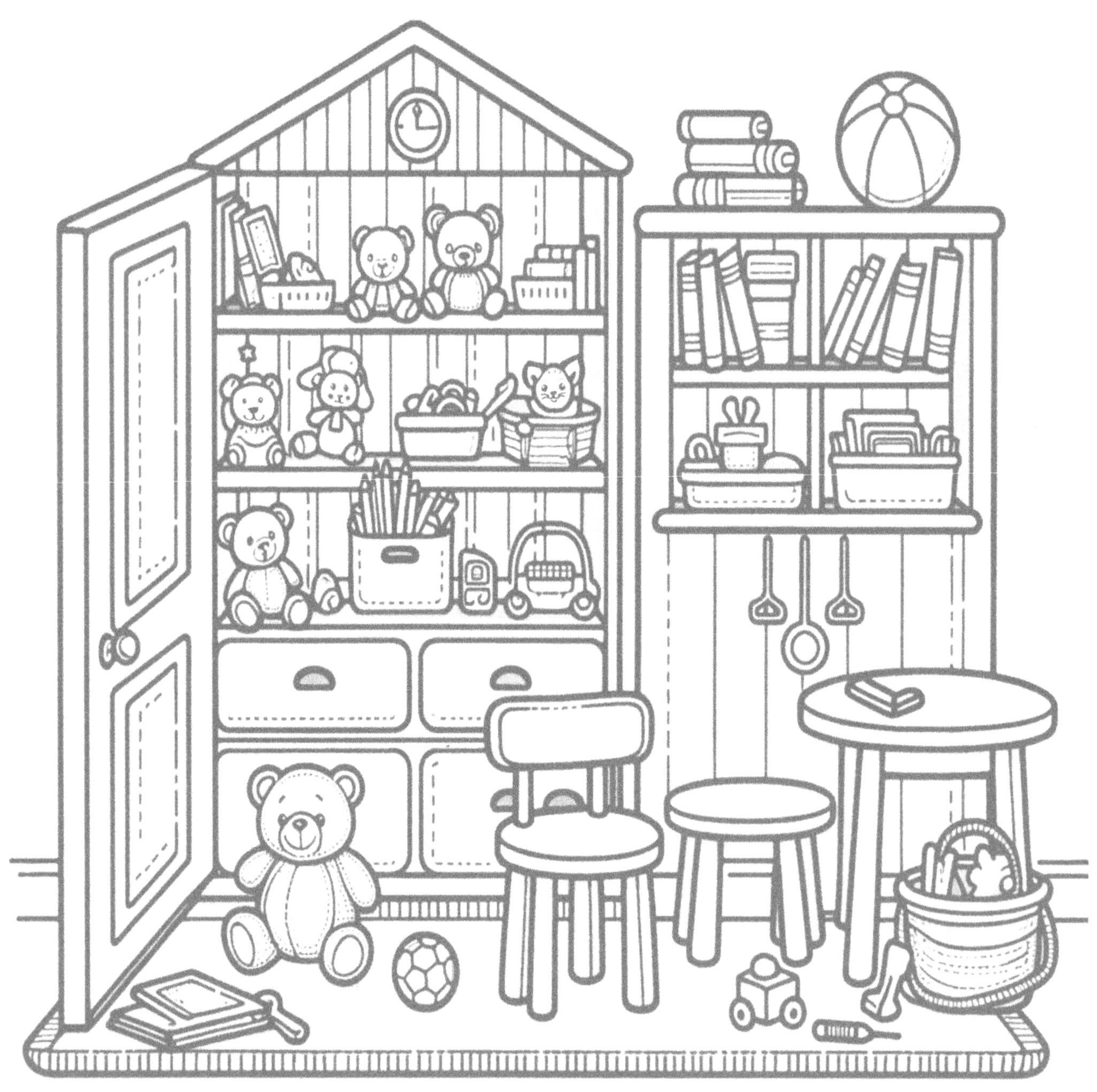

would you like to find the hidden cat hiding in this image & Color it??

Reflect on moments in your life when you thought you didn't have enough of something and felt the need to buy it, only to discover you already had it. List five such instances where you felt you were lacking or had lost something, but then found you always had it with you.

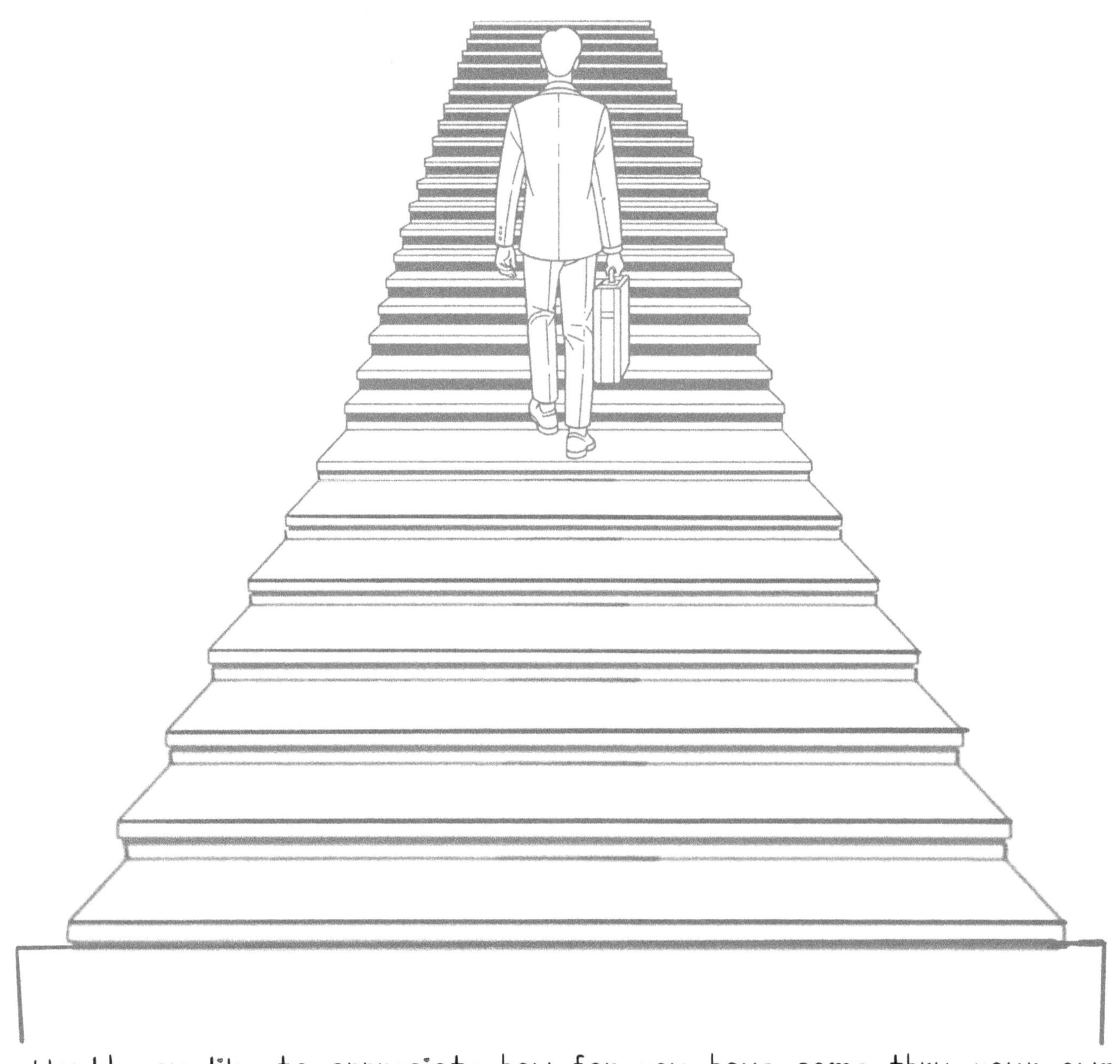

Would you like to appreciate how far you have come thru your own efforts & others help by coloring the image.

Would you like to list 5 points to appreciate your own efforts & others help ??

I always appreciate myself and others for their help for how far I have come

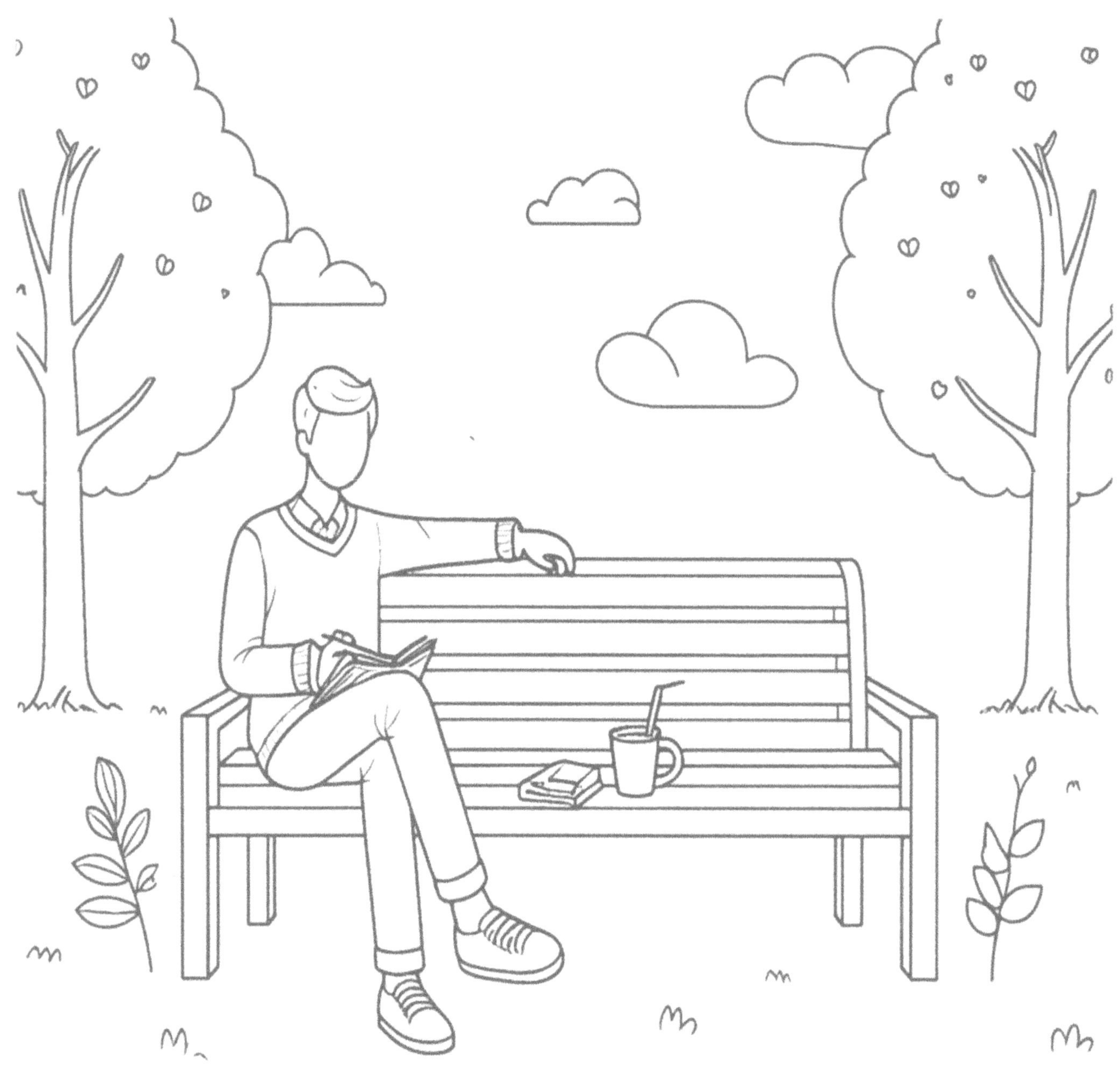

Would you like to appreciate the current moment by coloring the image?

Describe three small moments from today that brought you joy or contentment. Why did these moments stand out to you?

I appreciate each small moment

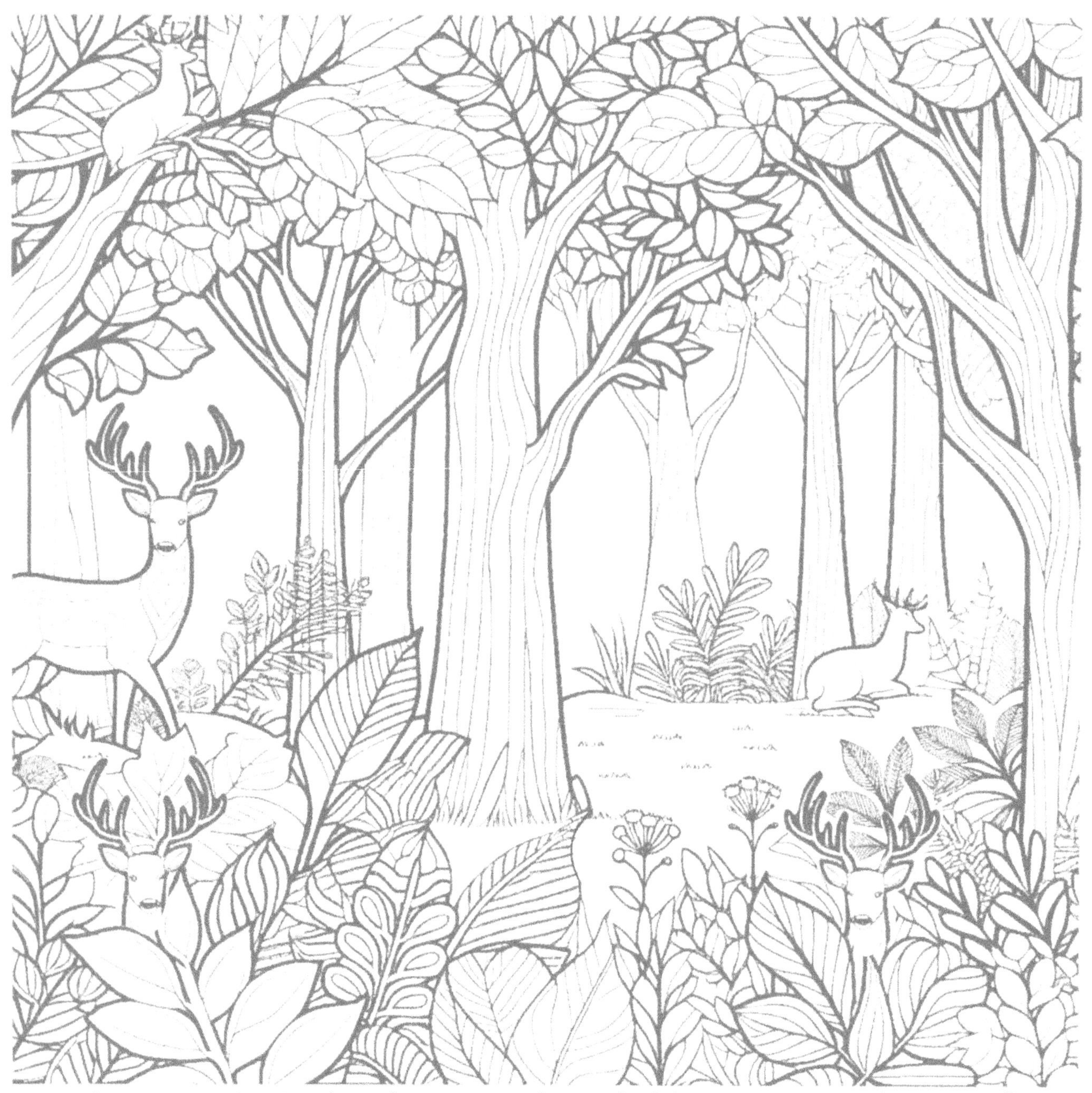

Would you like to find and color 5 deers hidden amongst the trees?

Reflect on a challenging situation you are currently facing. What positive aspects can you find in this challenge?

I find positive in every life situation & grow.

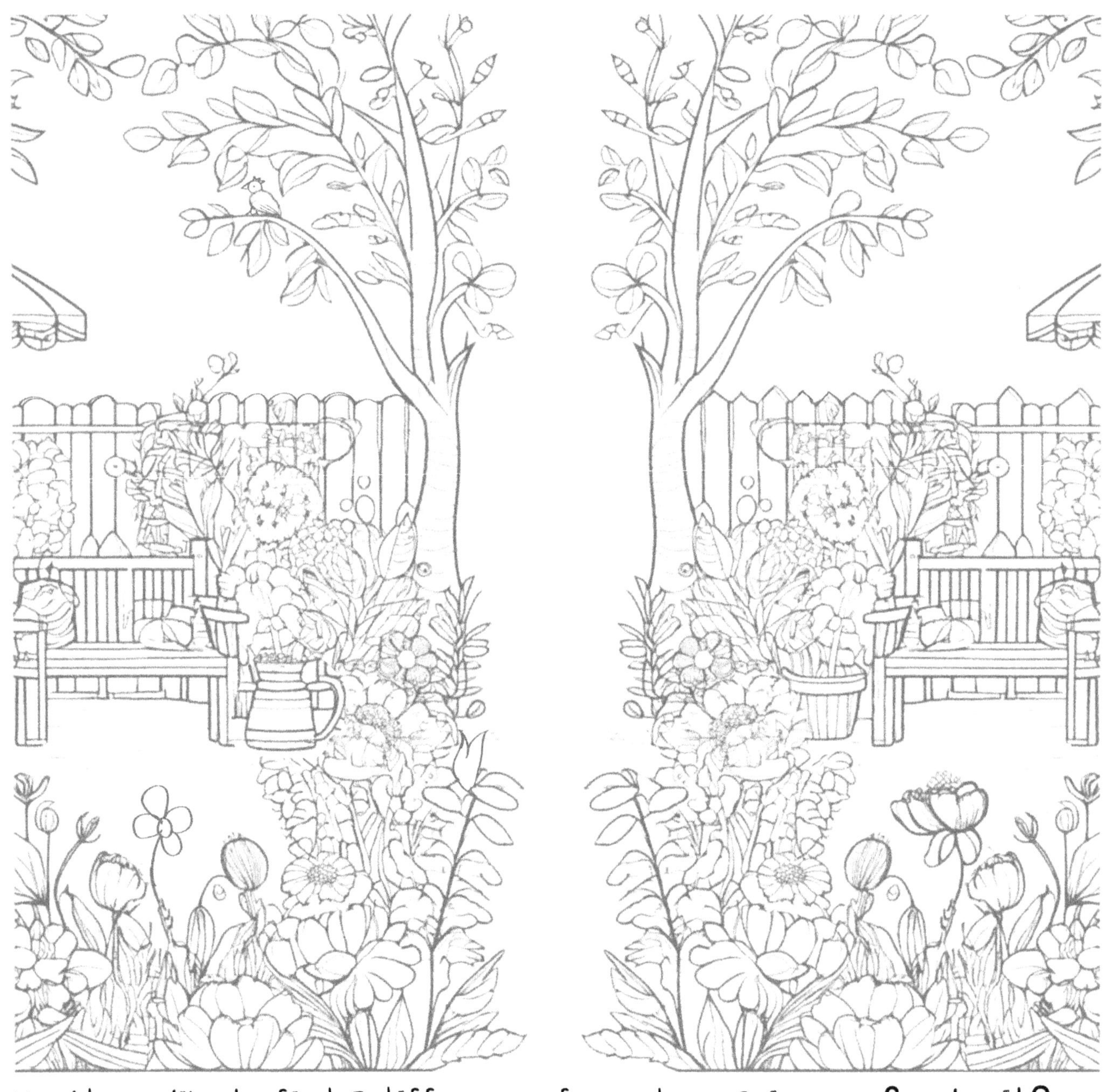

Would you like to find 5 differences from above 2 images & color it?

Could you spot 5 differences from now & before on how your reaction to the same life situation has changed?

I find positive in every life situation & grow.

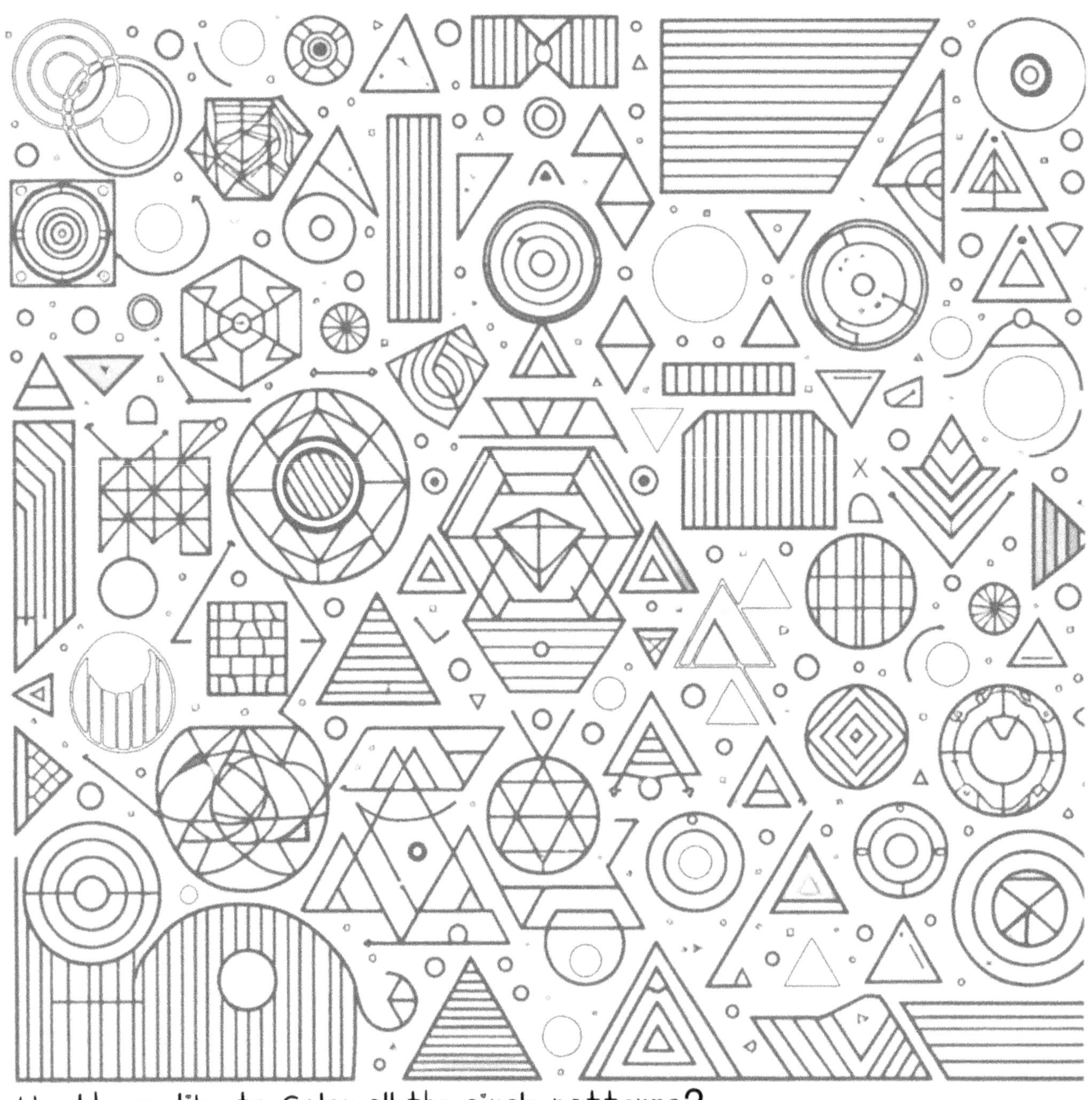

Would you like to Color all the circle patterns?

Reflect on life patterns that you have come out of ? Can you appreciate 5 life patterns you have broken ?

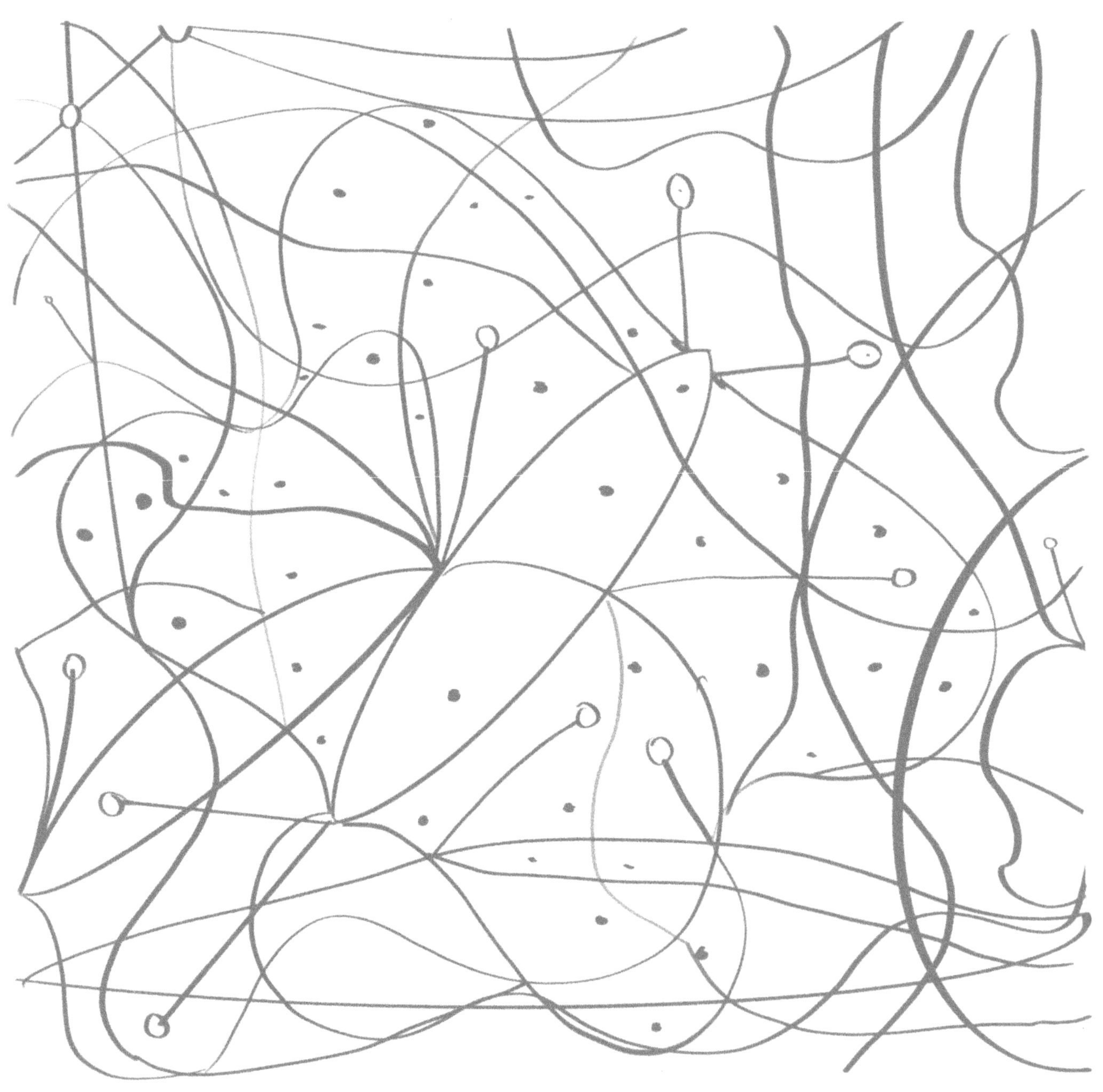

Would you like to fill in the colors to find hidden butterfly drawing ??

Reflect 5 such life moments, where you couldn't see the complete picture and still gave your best and kept patience & trust in your own abilities and universe ??

Appreciation, belief and trust in my own abilities and universe always reaps me happy fruits.

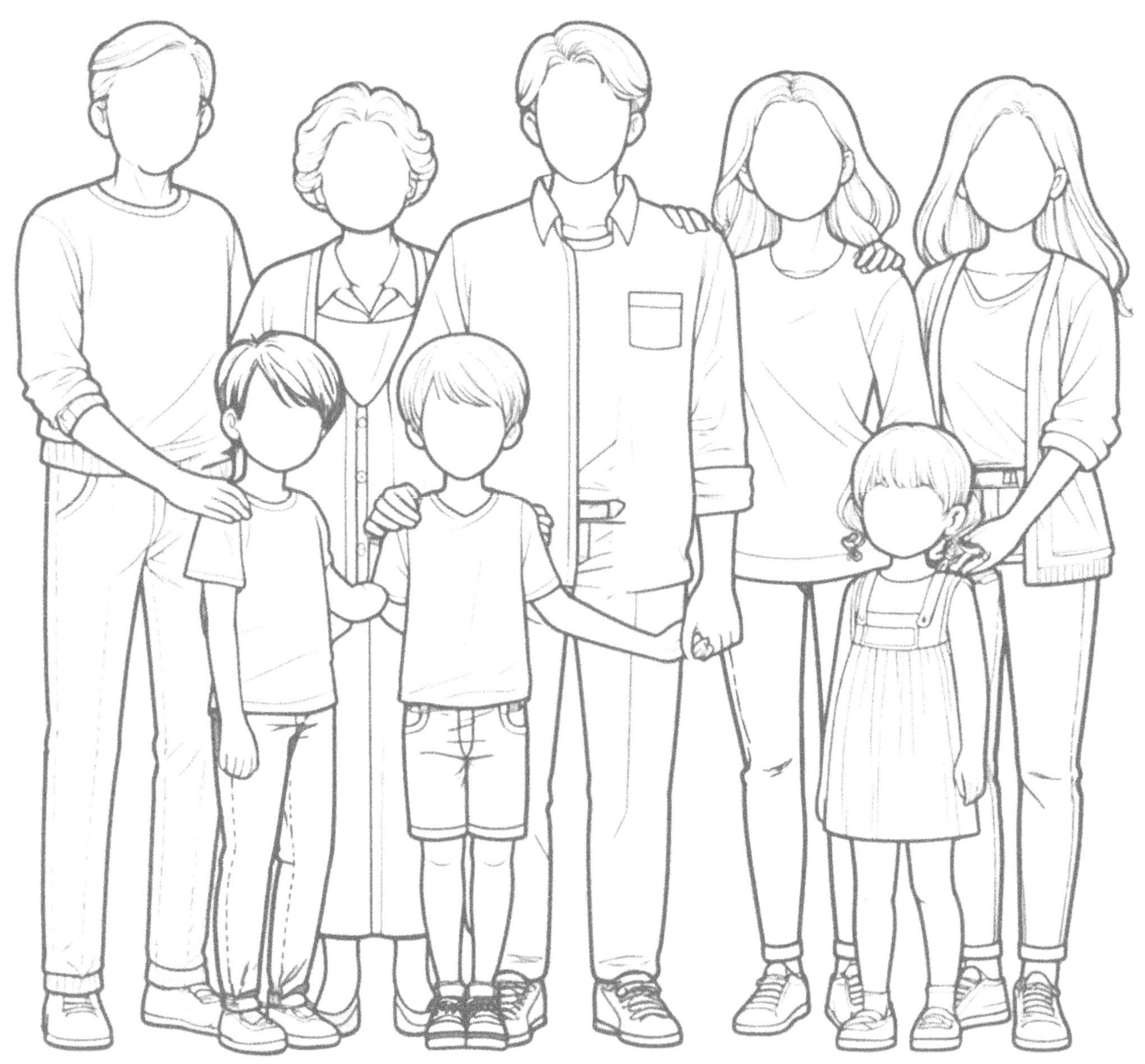

Can you name & draw face of people you know from your family & appreciate by coloring them ??

You have named people from your family and now could you find five ways to appreciate them ??

I always see good in others and that's what I always get.

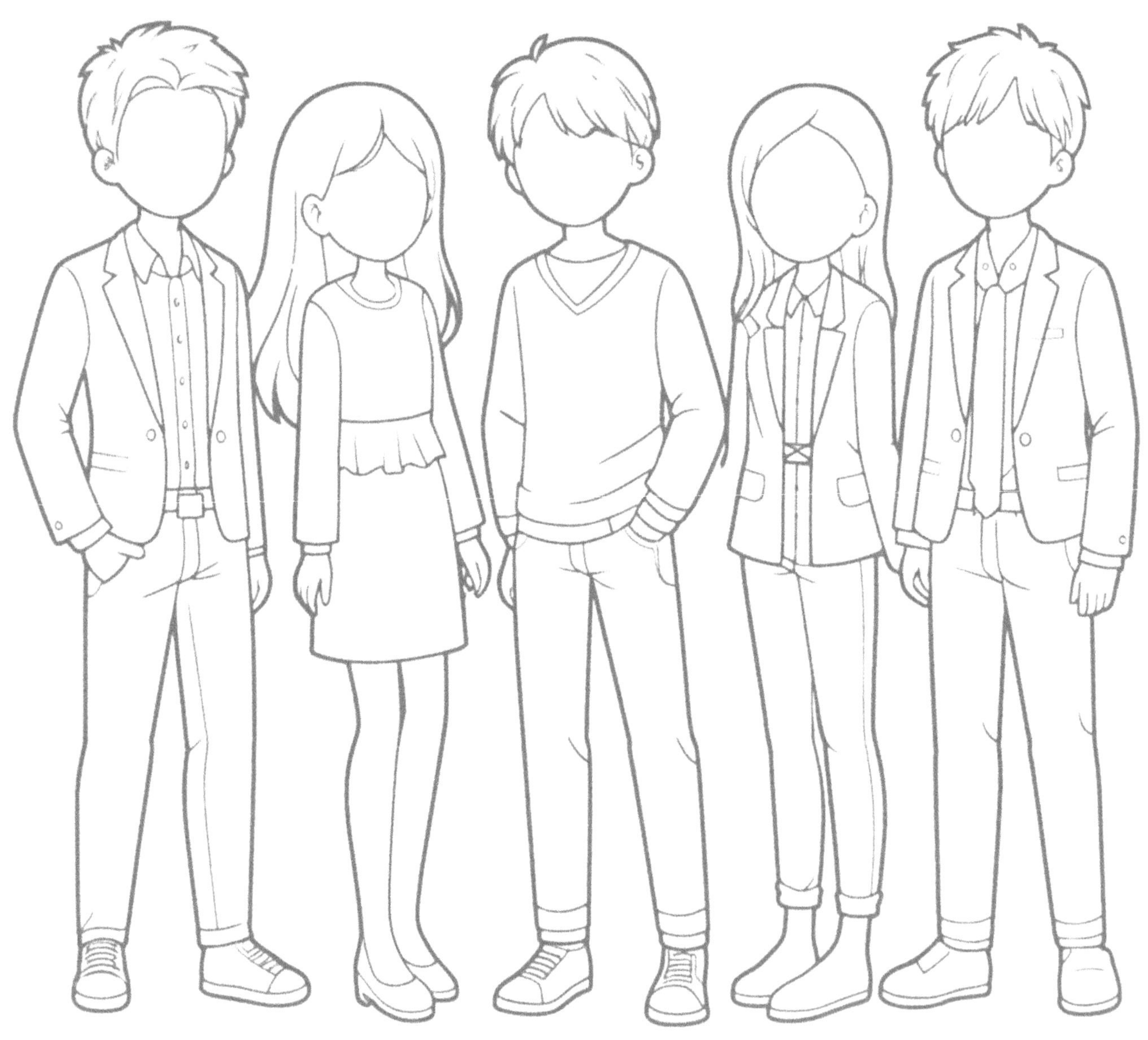

Can you name & draw face of people you know from your friends & colleagues, appreciate by coloring them ??

You have named people from your friends & colleagues and now could you find five ways you appreciate them ??

I always see good in others and that's what I always get.

Would you like to play, have fun and find your way start to finish? And color it too??

Would you list 5 moments you were busy having so much fun because you were in that moment present & aware? List 5 ways you can practice being in now and with full awareness ?

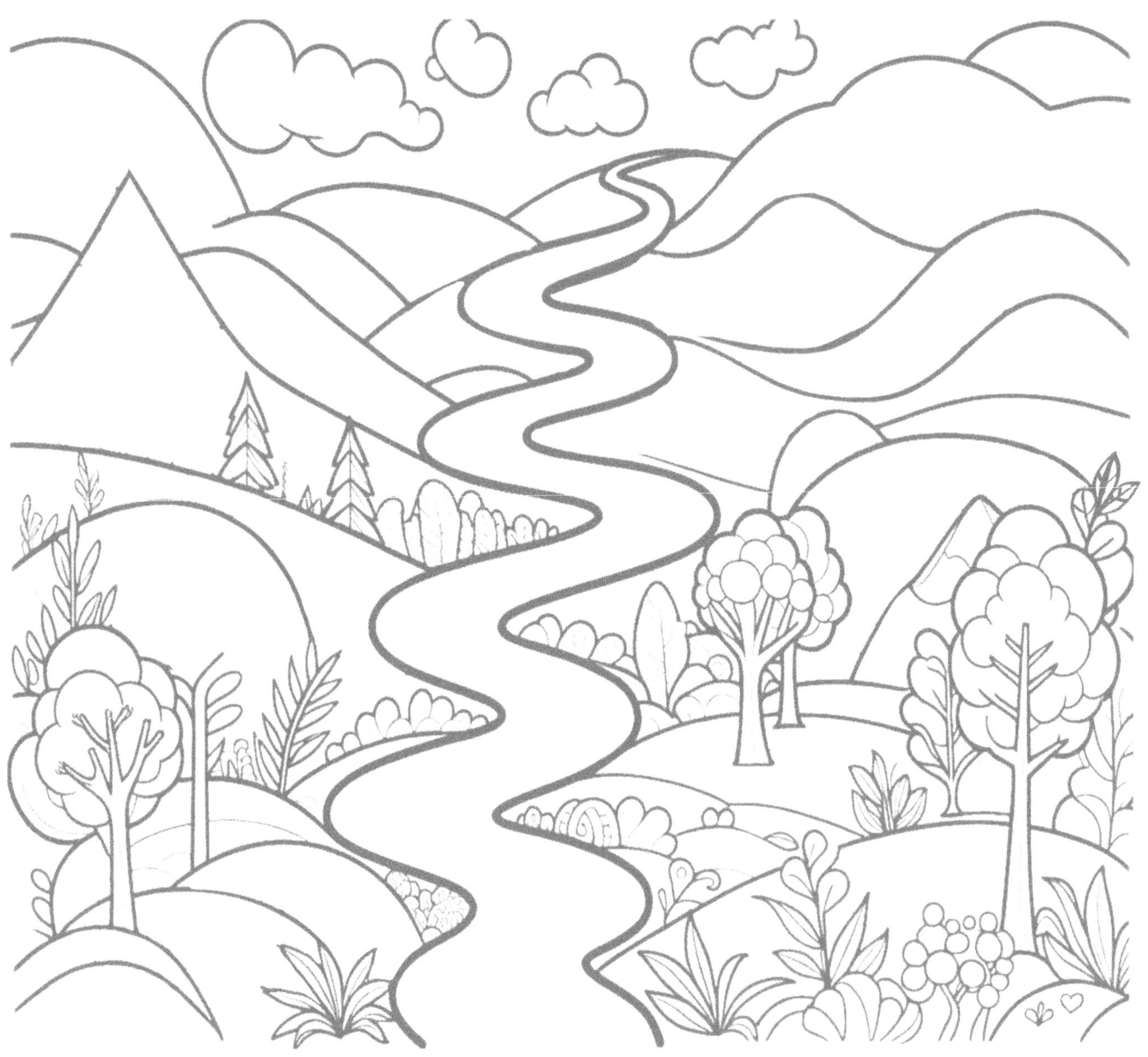

Would you like to doodle in empty paces & focus on the positive choices you made & just watch what comes?

Write about a positive choice you made this week.

I am proud of myself for the positive choices I make.

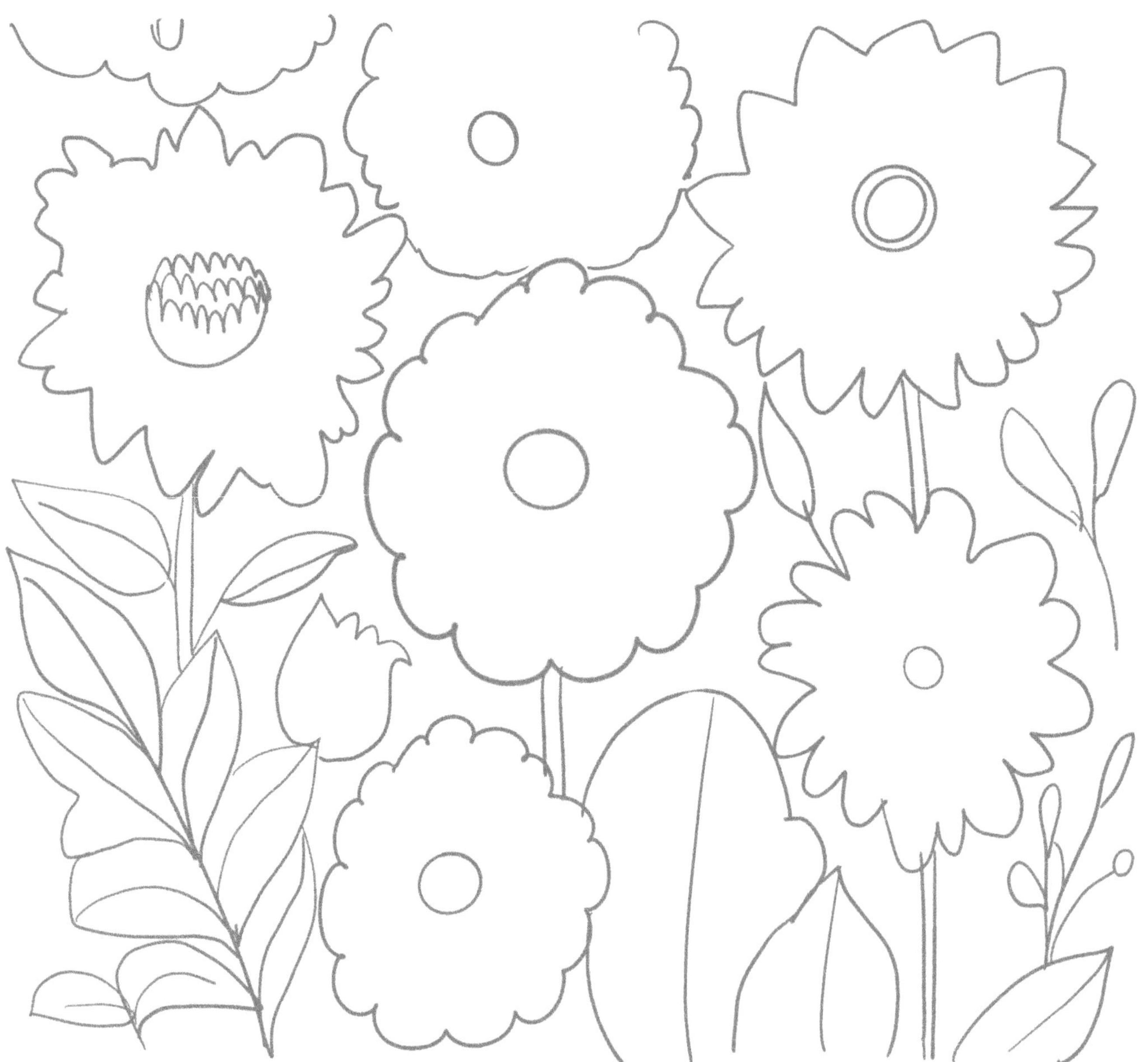

Would you like to doodle & watch your thoughts come & feel grateful or write in flowers something you're grateful for.

Create a gratitude list for today

Every day, I find reasons to appreciate life.

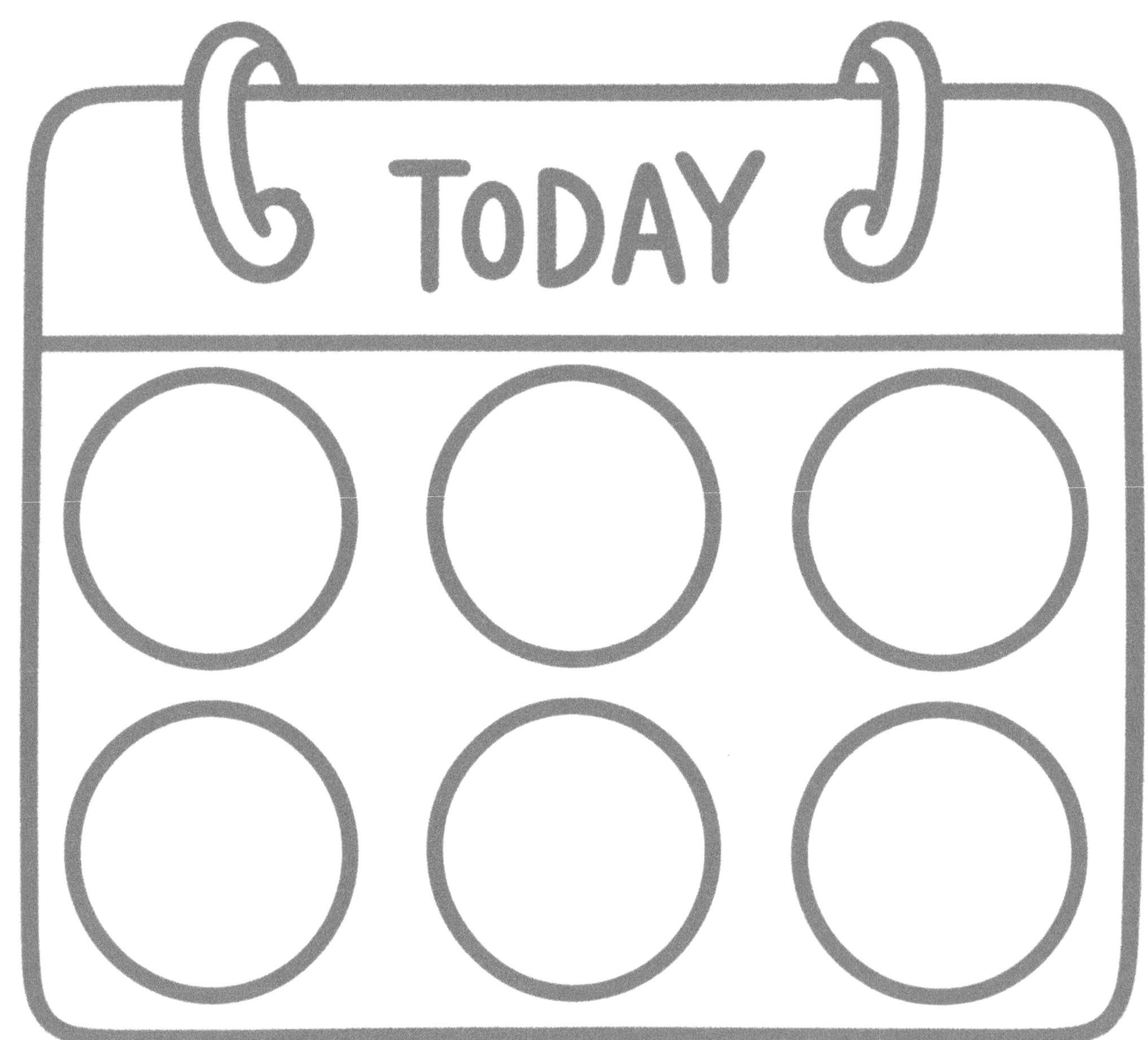

Would you like to doodle in above calendar & watch your thoughts as you remember good things that happened today ??

List 10 good things that happened today.

I see the good in every day.

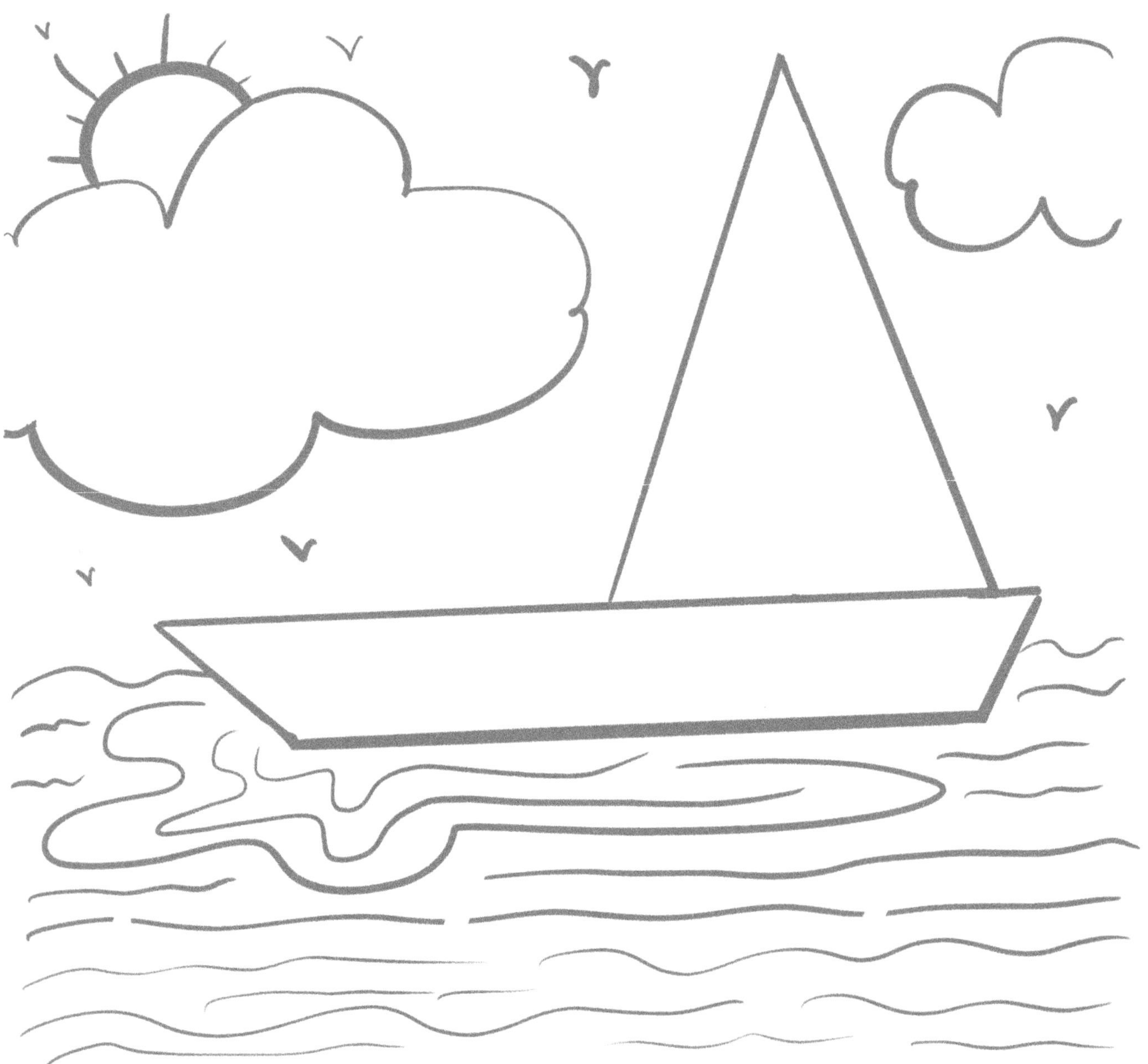

Would you like to doodle & watch your thoughts while you remember the beauty you saw around ??

Describe something beautiful you saw today?

I appreciate the beauty around me

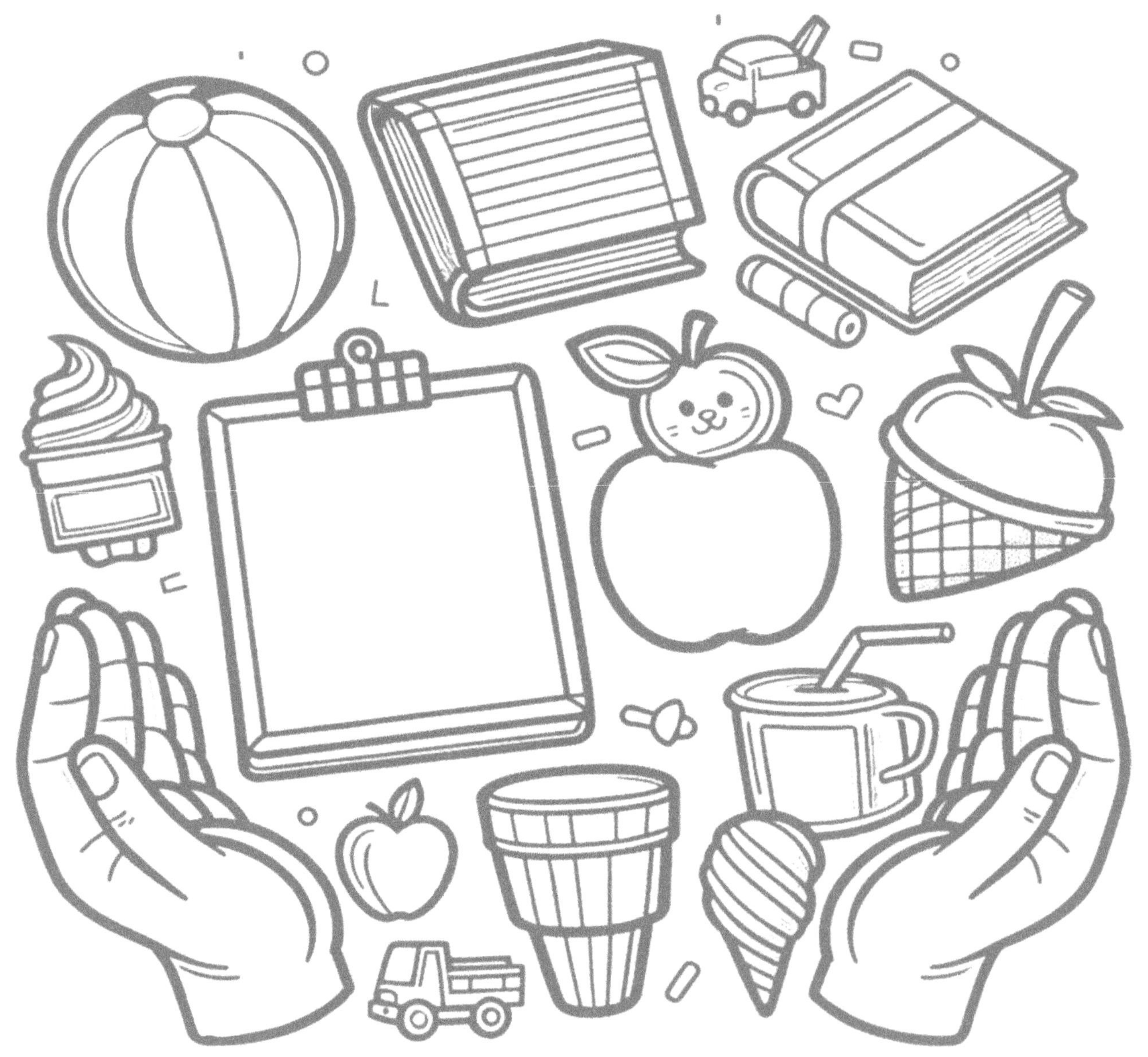

Would you like to doodle & watch your thoughts focus on things in your control ??

Write a list of things in your control ??

I focus on what I can control

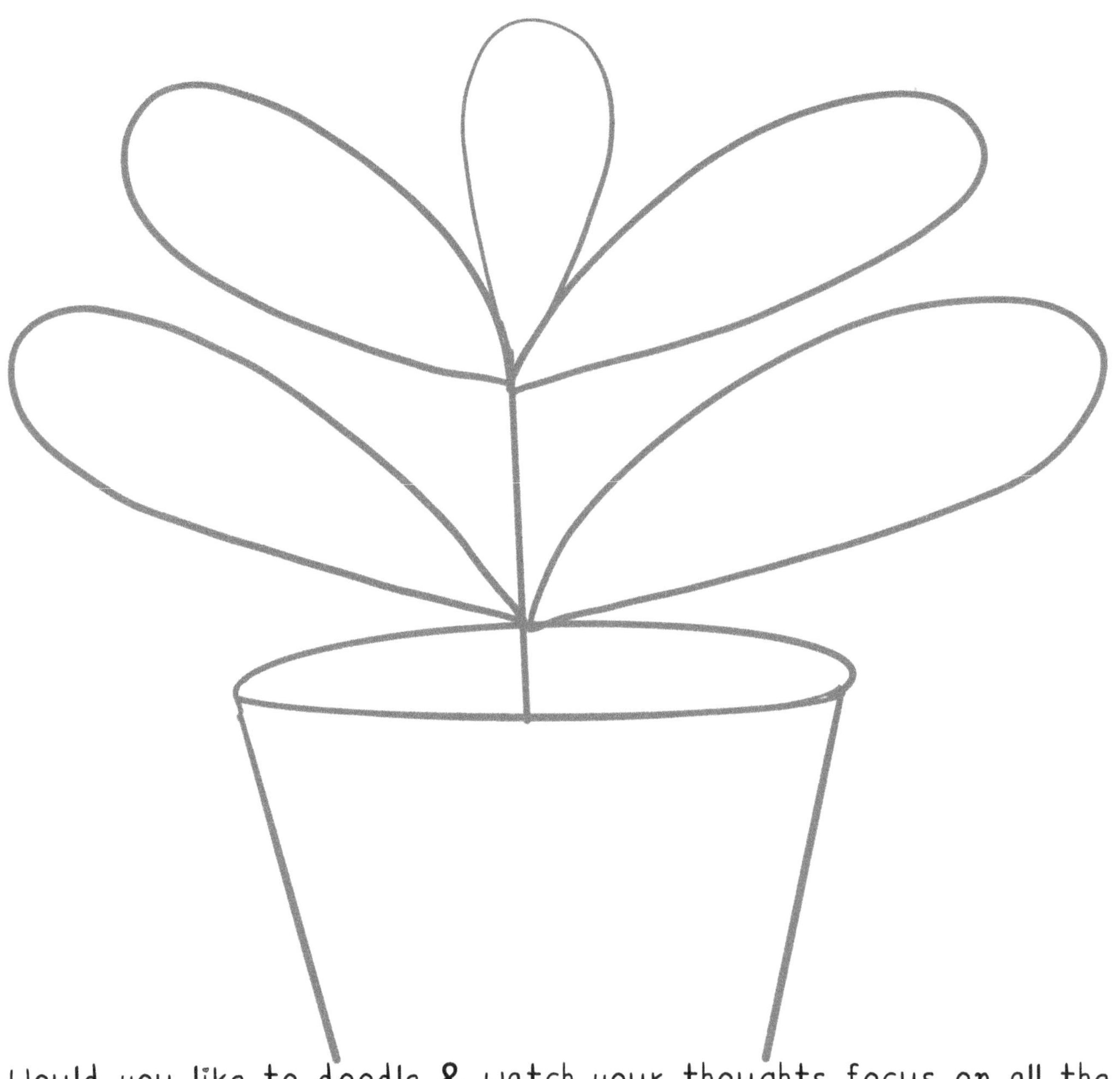

Would you like to doodle & watch your thoughts focus on all the opportunities you seized?

Describe an opportunity you seized.

I see opportunities for growth

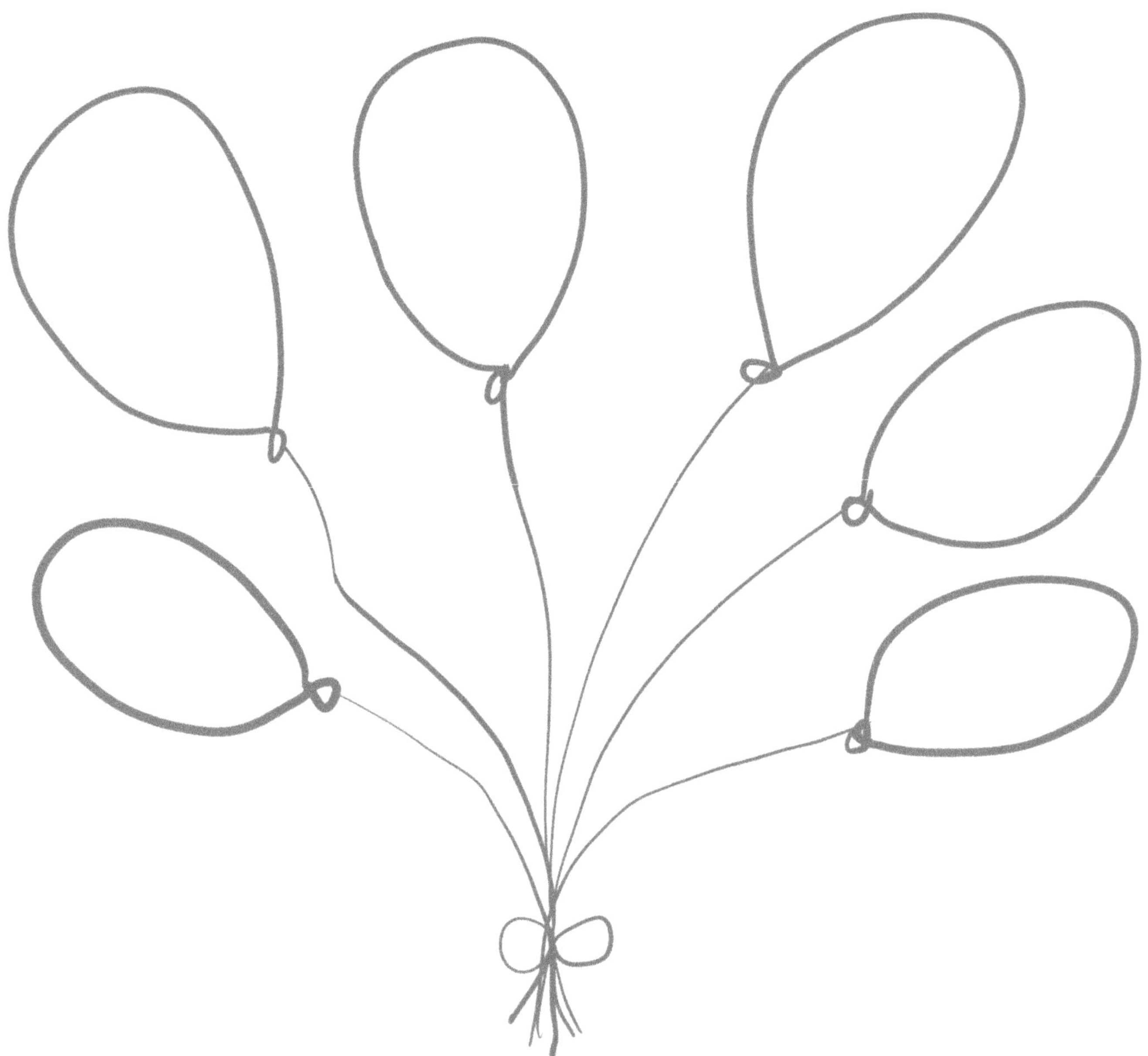

Would you like to doodle & watch your thoughts focus on all the moments of joy?

Reflect on a joyful moment from today

I appreciate moments of joy

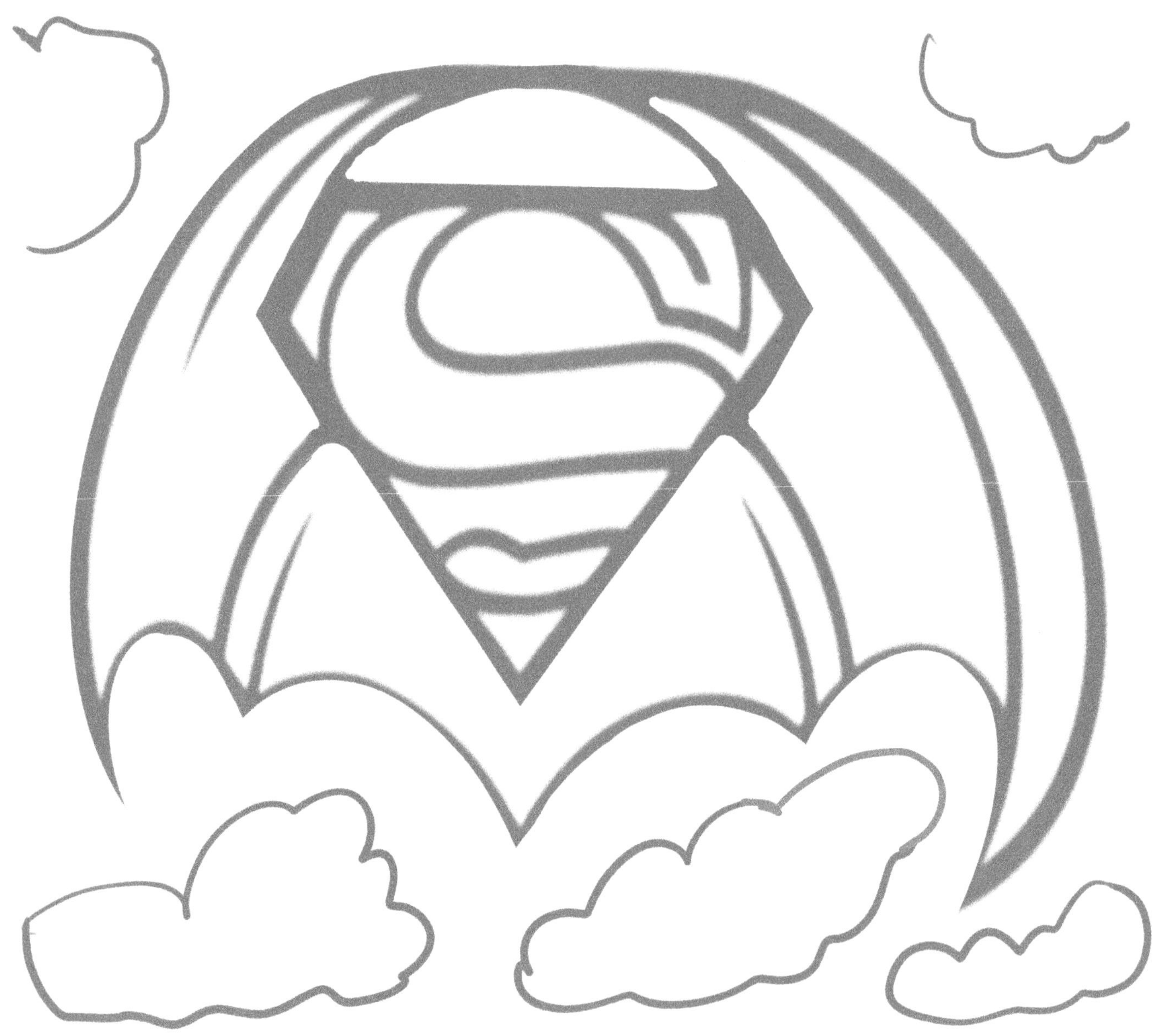

Would you like to doodle & watch your thoughts focus on all the things you are good at ??

Can you draw or write something you're good at?

I am confident in my abilities

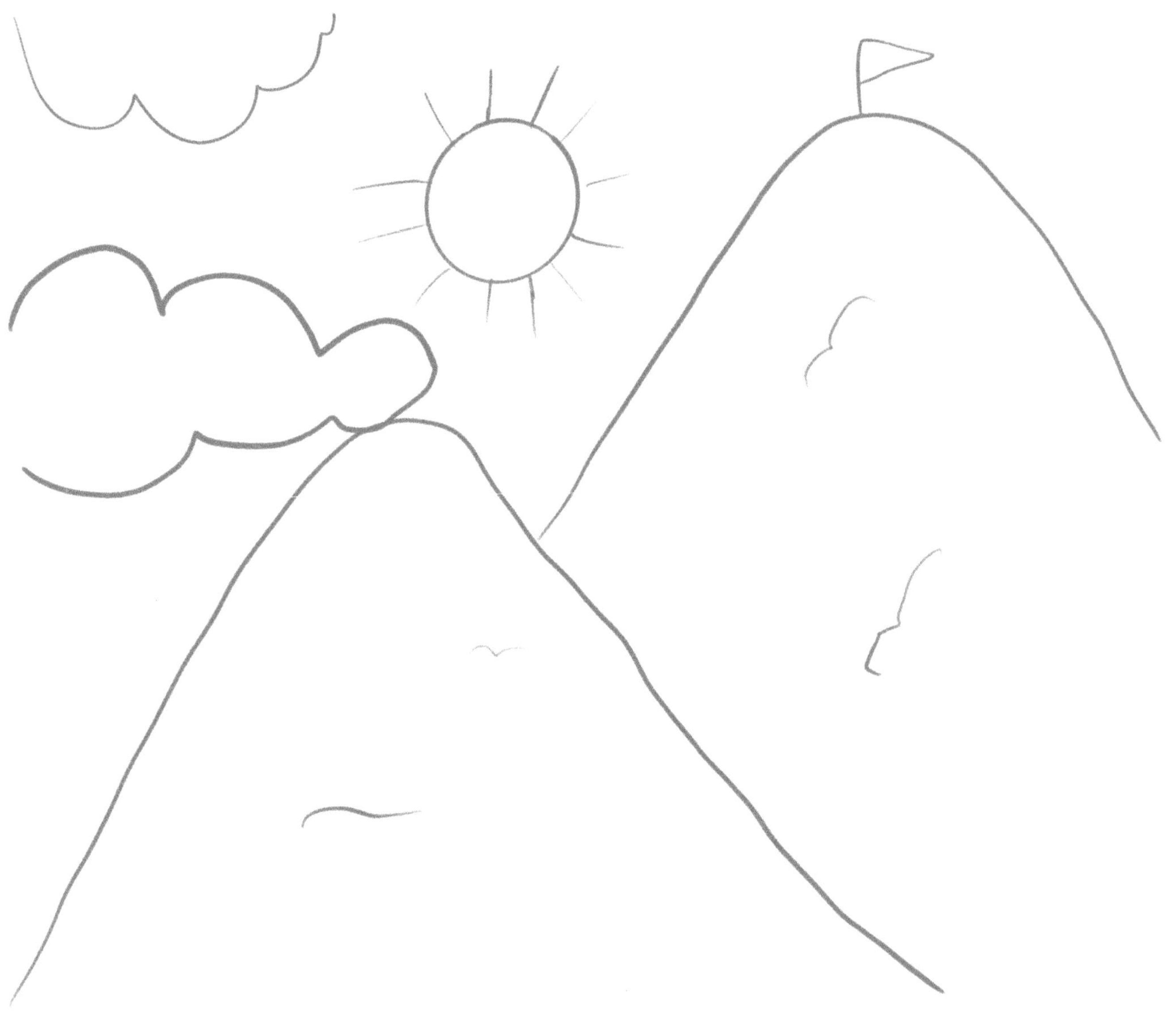

Would you like to doodle & watch your thoughts to appreciate your dedication & commitment ??

Write about a project you stayed committed to.

I appreciate my dedication

Would you like to doodle **&** watch your thoughts to appreciate your intuition **??**

Reflect on a time your instincts were right.

I trust my instincts

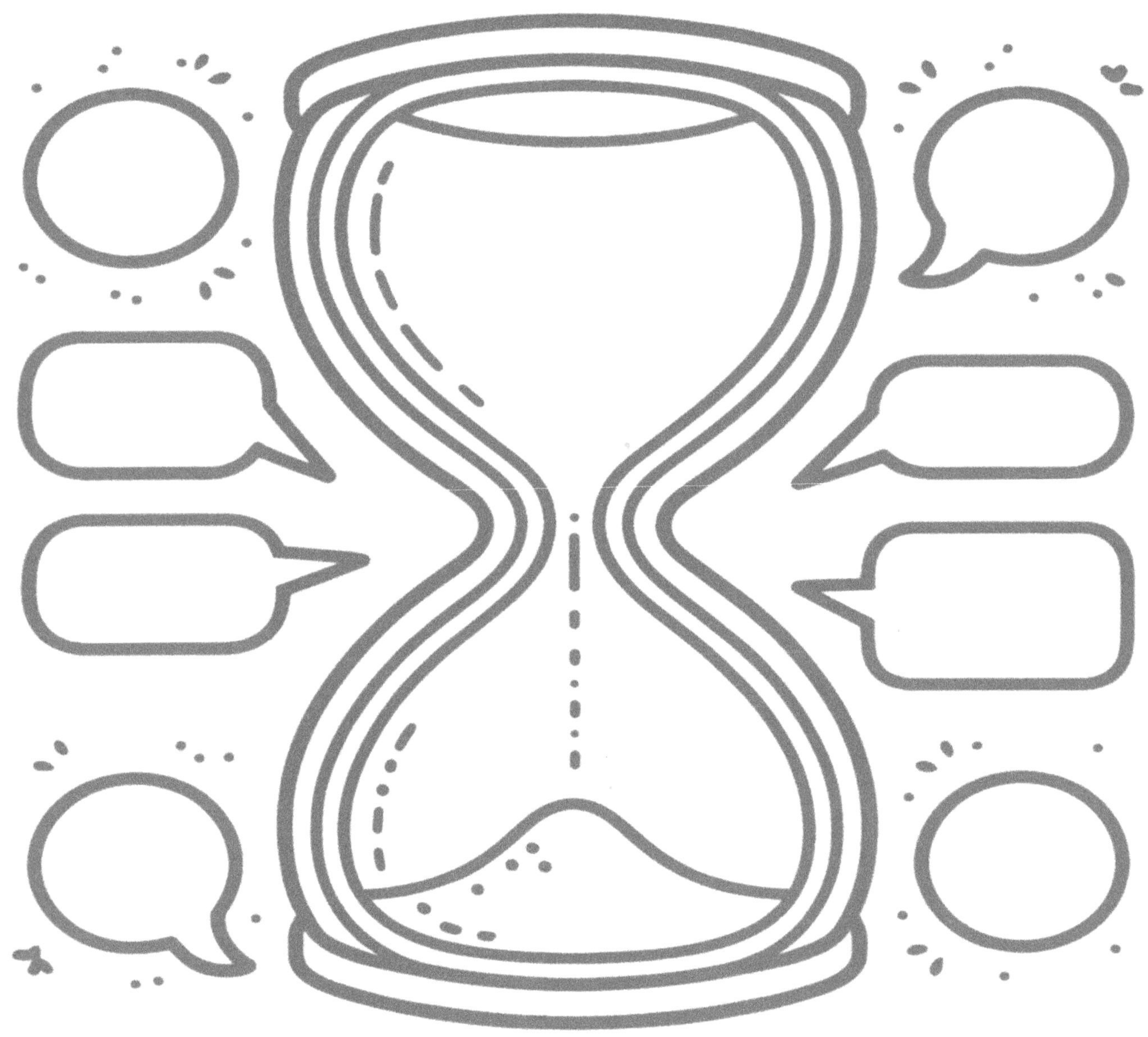

Would you like to doodle & watch your thoughts to appreciate how you use your time wisely ?

Write about how you used your time wisely this week.

I value my time

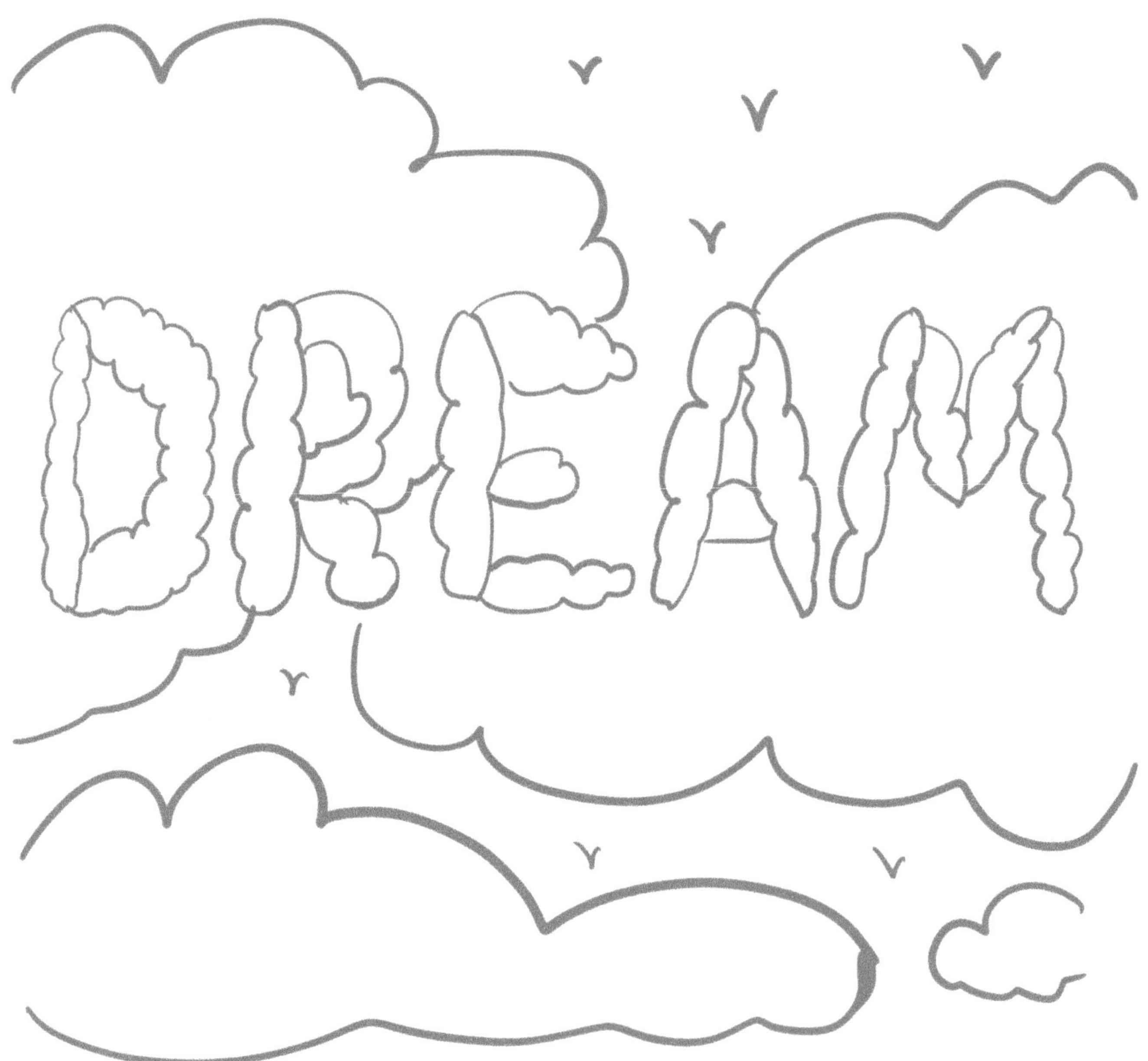

Would you like to doodle & watch your thoughts to appreciate how you made your biggest dream come true??

Draw your biggest dream coming true.

I am capable of great things

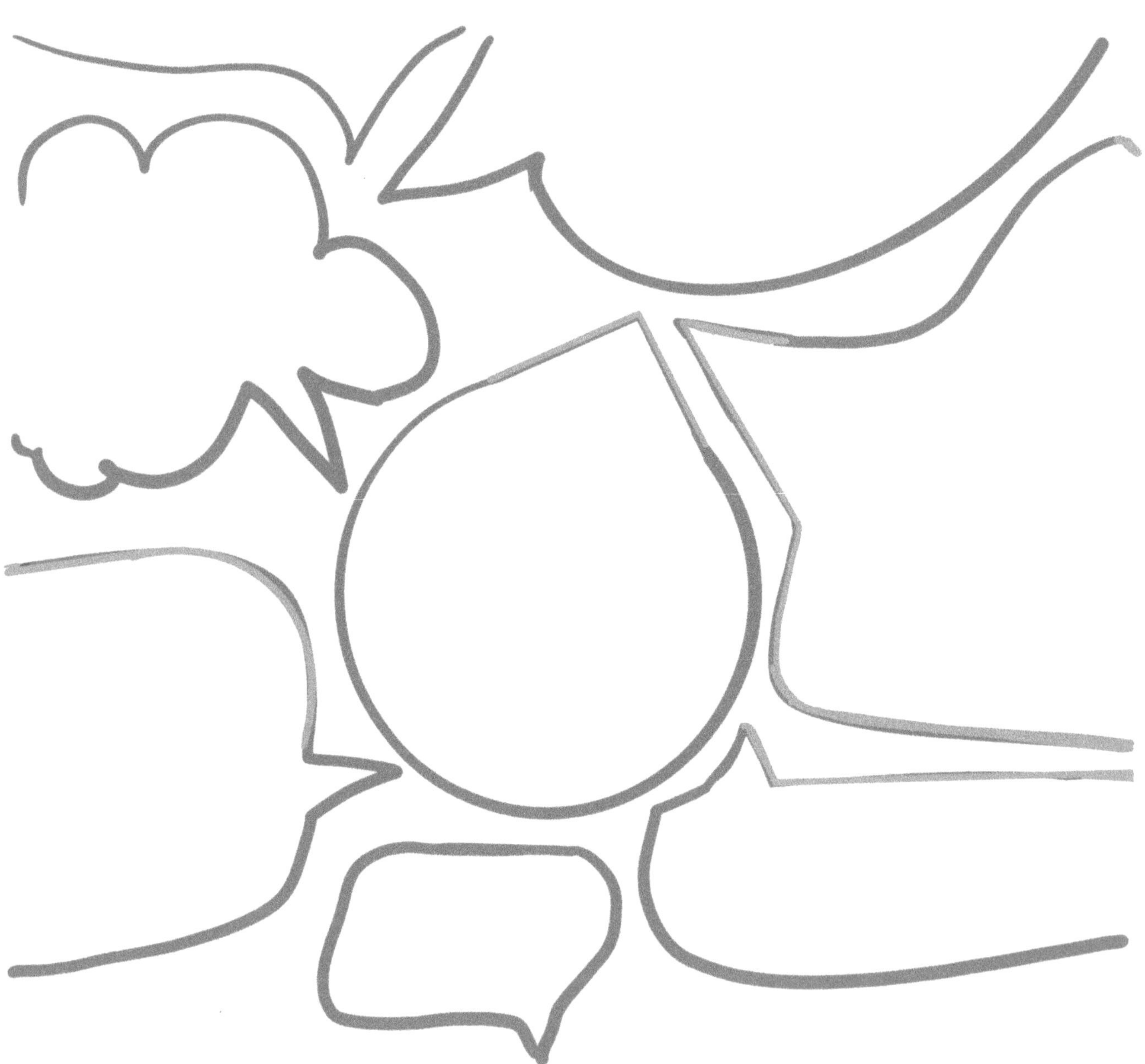

Would you like to doodle & watch your thoughts to appreciate all the compliments & praise you have received ??

Reflect on compliments you've received recently.

I am worthy of praise

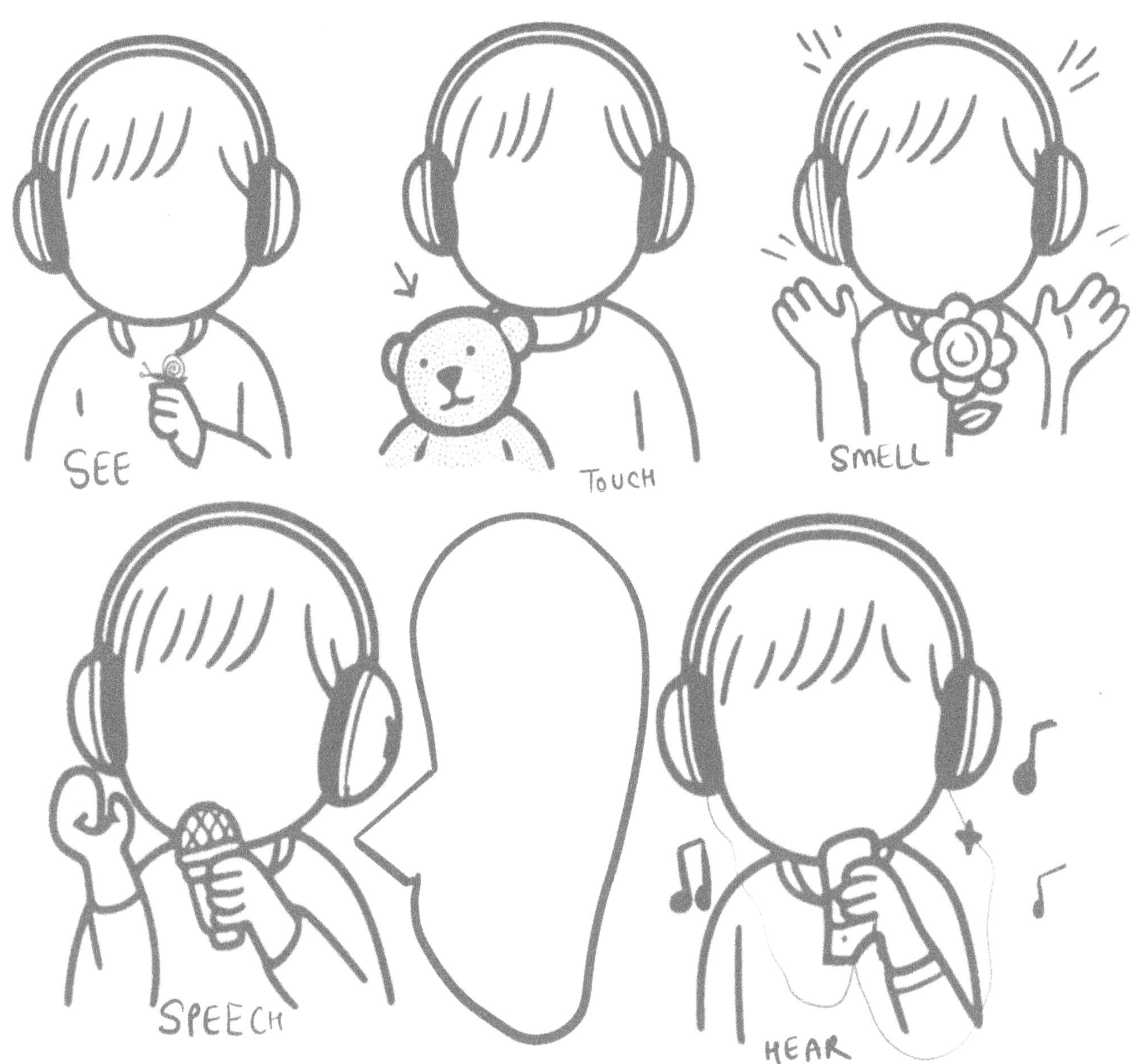

Would you like to doodle & watch your thoughts to appreciate your senses that can see, hear, speech, smell & touch?

Describe the sounds, sights, and smells around you right now. List 10 ways 5 senses are helping you.

I am aware of my surroundings

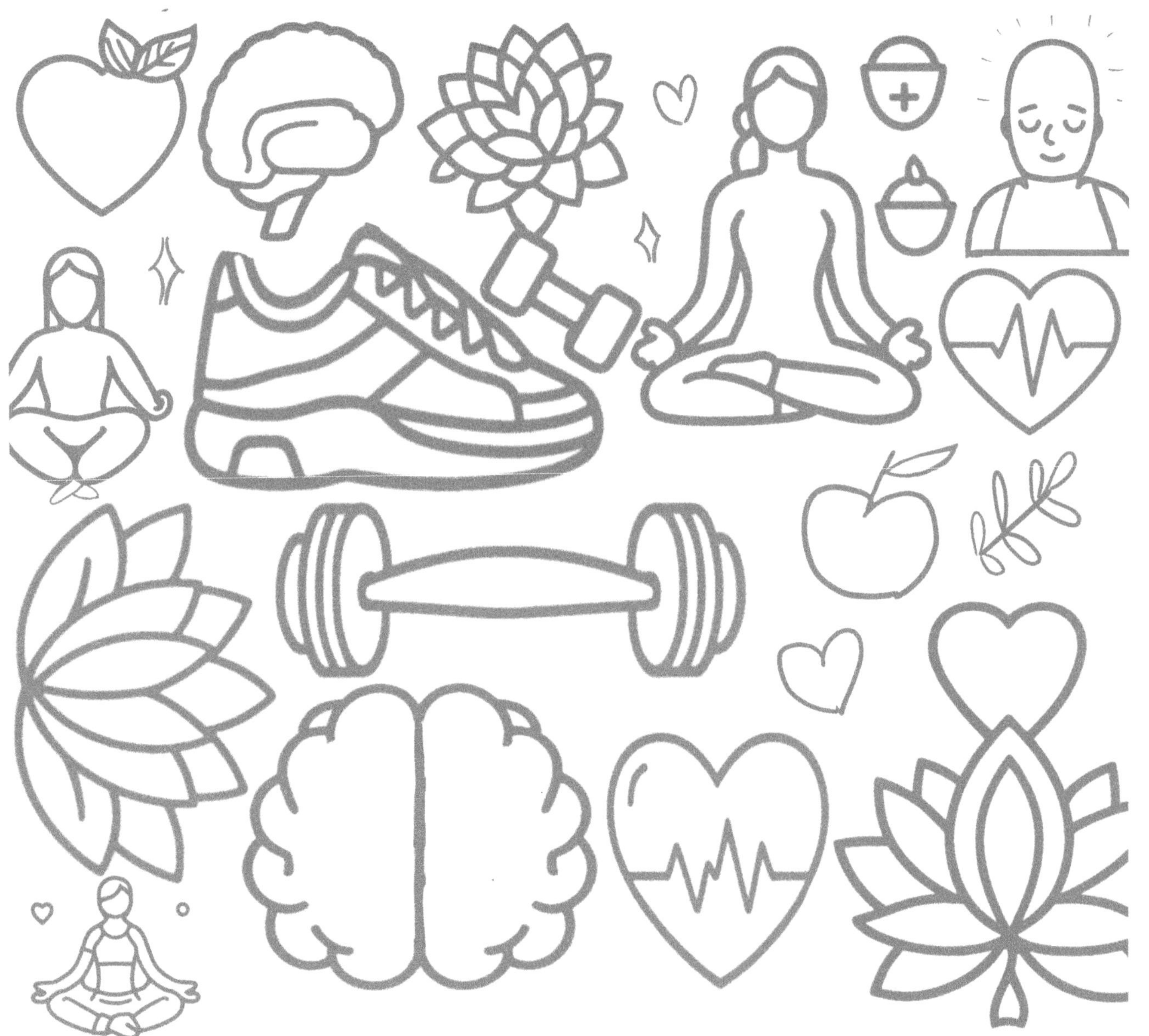

Would you like to doodle & watch your thoughts to appreciate yourself to take care of your self (physically, mentally & spiritually)?

Draw or write 10 ways you take care of yourself.

I am able to take care of myself